A Key Into the Language of America

ROGER WILLIAMS

COSIMOCLASSICS

NEW YORK

A Key Into the Language of America
Cover Copyright © 2009 by Cosimo, Inc.

A Key Into the Language of America was originally published in 1643.

For information, address:
P.O. Box 416, Old Chelsea Station
New York, NY 10011

or visit our website at:
www.cosimobooks.com

Ordering Information:
Cosimo publications are available at online bookstores. They may
also be purchased for educational, business or promotional use:
- *Bulk orders:* special discounts are available on bulk orders for reading
groups, organizations, businesses, and others. For details contact
Cosimo Special Sales at the address above or at info@cosimobooks.com.
- *Custom-label orders:* we can prepare selected books with your cover or
logo of choice. For more information, please contact Cosimo at
info@cosimobooks.com.

Cover Design by www.popshopstudio.com

ISBN: 978-1-61640-304-1

"It is a strange *truth*, that a man shall generally finde
more free entertainment and refreshing amongst these
Barbarians, than amongst thousands that call themselves
Christians.

—from "The observation generall from their eating, &c." p.16

To my Deare and Welbeloved
Friends *and* Countrey-men, *in old and new* ENGLAND.

Present you with a *Key*; I have not heard of the like, yet framed, since it pleased God to bring that mighty *Continent* of *America* to light: Others of my Countreymen have often, and excellently, and lately written of the *Countrey* (and none that I know beyond the goodnesse and worth of it.)

This *Key*, respects the *Native Language* of it, and happily may unlocke some *Rarities* concerning the *Natives* themselves, not yet discovered.

I drew the *Materialls* in a rude lumpe at Sea, as a private *helpe* to my owne memory, that I might not by my present ab-

A 2   sence

To the Reader.

sence *lightly lose* what I had so *dearely bought* in some few yeares *hardship*, and *charges* among the *Barbarians*; yet being reminded by some, what pitie it were to bury those *Materialls* in my *Grave* at land or Sea; and withall, remembring how oft I have been importun'd by *worthy friends*, of all sorts, to afford them some helps this way.

I resolved (by the assistance of *the most High*) to cast those *Materialls* into this *Key*, *pleasant* and *profitable* for *All*, but specially for my *friends* residing in those parts:

A little *Key* may open a *Box*, where lies a *bunch* of *Keyes*.

With this I have entred into the secrets of those *Countries*, where ever *English* dwel about two hundred miles, betweene the *French* and *Dutch* Plantations; for want of this, I know what grosse mis-takes my selfe and others have run into.

There is a mixture of this *Language* North and *South*, from the place of my abode, about six hundred miles; yet within the two hundred miles (aforementi-
oned)

oned) their *Dialects* doe exceedingly dif-
fer; yet not so, but (within that compasse)
a man may, by this *helpe,* converse with
thousands of *Natives* all over the *Countrey*:
and by such converse it may please the *Father* of *Mercies* to spread *civilitie,* (and in
his owne most holy season) *Christianitie*;
for *one Candle* will light *ten thousand,* and
it may please *God* to blesse a *little Leaven*
to season the *mightie Lump* of those *Peoples*
and *Territories.*

It is expected, that having had so much
converse with these *Natives,* I should write
some litle of them.

Concerning them (a little to gratifie
expectation) I shall touch upon *foure
Heads:*

First, by what *Names* they are distinguished.

Secondly, Their *Originall* and *Descent.*

Thirdly, their *Religion, Manners, Customes,* &c.

Fourthly, That great *Point* of their *Conversion.*

To the first, their *Names* are of two
sorts: A 3   First,

To the Reader.

First, those of the *English* giving: as *Natives, Salvages, Indians, Wild-men,* (so the *Dutch* call them *Wilden*) *Abergeny men, Pagans, Barbarians, Heathen.*

Secondly, their *Names,* which they give themselves.

I cannot observe, that they ever had (before the comming of the *English, French* or *Dutch* amongst them) any *Names* to difference *themselves* from strangers, for they knew none; but two sorts of *names* they had, and have amongst *themselves.*

First, *generall,* belonging to all *Natives,* as *Ninnuock, Ninnimissinnûwock, Eniskeetompaûwog,* which signifies *Men, Folke,* or *People.*

Secondly, particular *names,* peculiar to severall *Nations,* of them amongst *themselves,* as, *Nanhigganēuck, Massachusêuck, Cawasumsêuck, Cowwesêuck, Quintikóock, Qunnipiēuck, Pequttóog,* &c.

They have often asked mee, why wee call them *Indians Natives,* &c. And understanding the reason, they will call themselues *Indians,* in opposition to *English,* &c.   For

For the second Head proposed, their *Originall* and *Descent.*

From *Adam* and *Noah* that they spring, it is granted on all hands.

But for their later *Descent,* and whence they came into those pars, it seemes as hard to finde, as to finde the *wellhead* of some fresh *Streame,* which running many miles out of the *Countrey* to the salt *Ocean,* hath met with many mixing *Streames* by the way. They say themselves, that they have sprung and growne up in that very place, like the very *trees* of the *wildernesse.*

They say that their *Great God Cawtán-towwit* created those parts, as I observed in the Chapter of their *Religion.* They have no *Clothes, Bookes,* nor *Letters,* and conceive their *Fathers* never had; and therefore they are easily perswaded that the *God* that made *English* men is a greater *God,* because Hee hath so richly endowed the *English* above *themselves* : But when they heare that about sixteen hundred yeeres agoe, *England* and the *Inhabitants* thereof were like unto *themselves,*

A 4   and

and since have received from *God, Clothes, Bookes,* &c. they are greatly affected with a secret hope concerning *themselves.*

Wise and *Judicious* men, with whom I have discoursed, maintaine their *Originall* to be *Northward* from *Tartaria:* and at my now taking ship, at the *Dutch Plantation,* it pleased the *Dutch* Governour, (in some discourse with mee about the *Natives*), to draw their *Line* from *Iceland,* because the name *Sackmakan* (the name for an *Indian* Prince, about the *Dutch*) is the name for a *Prince* in *Iceland.*

Other opinions I could number up: under favour I shall present (not mine opinion, but) my *Observations* to the judgement of the Wise.

First, others (and my selfe) have conceived some of their words to hold affinitie with the *Hebrew.*

Secondly, they constantly *annoint* their *heads* as the *Jewes* did.

Thirdly, they give *Dowries* for their wives, as the *Jewes* did.

Fourthly (and which I have not so ob-

serued

served amongst other *Nations* as amongst the *Jewes,* and *these:*) they constantly seperate their Women (during the time of their monthly sicknesse) in a little house alone by themselves foure or five dayes, and hold it an *Irreligious thing* for either *Father* or *Husband* or any *Male* to come neere them.

They have often asked me if it bee so with *women* of other *Nations,* and whether they are so *separated:* and for their practice they plead *Nature* and *Tradition.* Yet againe I have found a greater *Affinity* of their Language with the *Greek* Tongue.

2. As the *Greekes* and other *Nations,* and our selves call the seven *Starres* (or Charles Waine the *Beare,*) so doe they *Mosk* or *Paukunnawaw* the Beare.

3. They have many strange Relations of one *Wétucks,* a man that wrought great *Miracles* amongst them, and *walking upon tho waters,*, &c. with some kind of broken Resemblance to the *Sonne of God.*

Lastly, it is famous that the *Sowwest* (*Sowaniu*) is the great Subject of their dis-

course.

course. From thence their *Traditions.* There they say (at the *South-west*) is the Court of their *great God Cautántouwit:* At *the South-west* are their *Forefathers* soules: *to the South-west* they goe themselves when they dye; From the *South-west* came their *Corne,* and Beanes out of their Great *God Cautántowwits* field: And indeed the further *Northward* and *Westward* from us their Corne will not grow, but to the *Southward* better and better. I dare not conjecture in these *Vncertainties,* I believe they are *lost,* and yet hope (in the Lords holy season) some of the wildest of them shall be found to share in the blood of the Son of God. To the third *Head,* concerning their *Religion, Customes, Manners* &c. I shall here say nothing, because in those 32. Chapters of the whole Book, I have briefly touched those of all sorts, from their *Birth* to their *Burialls,* and have endeavoured (as the Nature of the worke would give way) to bring some short *Observations* and *Applications* home to *Europe* from *America.*

Therefore

Therefore fourthly, to that great Point of their Conversion so much to bee longed for, and by all *New-English* so much pretended, and I hope in Truth.

For my selfe I have uprightly laboured to suite my endeavours to my pretences: and of later times (out of desire to attaine their Language) I have run through varieties of *Intercourses* with them Day and Night, Summer and Winter, by Land and Sea, particular passages tending to this, I have related divers, in the Chapter of their Religion.

Many solemne discourses I have had with all *sorts of Nations* of them, from one end of the Countrey to another (so farre as opportunity, and the little Language I have could reach.)

I know there is no small *preparation* in the hearts of Multitudes of them. I know their many solemne *Confessions* to my self, and one to another of their lost *wandring Conditions.*

I know strong *Convictions* upon the *Consciences* of many of them, and their desires uttred that way.   I

To the Reader.

I know not with how little *Knowledge* and *Grace* of Christ the Lord may save, and therefore neither will *despaire*, nor *report* much.

But since it hath pleased some of my Worthy *Country-men* to mention (of late in print) *VVequash*, the *Péqut Captaine*, I shall be bold so farre to second their *Relations*, as to relate mine owne Hopes of Him (though I dare not be so confident as others.

Two dayes before his Death, as I past up to *Qunnibticut* River, it pleased my worthy friend Mr. *Fenwick* whom I visited at his house in *Say-Brook* Fort at the mouth of that River) to tell me that my old friend *VVequash* lay very sick: I desired to see him, and Himselfe was pleased to be my Guide two mile where *VVequash* lay.

Amongst other discourse conccrning his *sicknesse* and *Death* (in which hee freely bequeathed his son to Mr. *Fenwick*) I closed with him concerning his *Soule:* Hee told me that some two or three yeare before

fore he had lodged at my House, where I acquainted him with the *Condition* of *all mankind*, & his *Own* in particular, how *God* created *Man* and *Allthings* : how *Man* fell from *God*, and of his present *Enmity* against *God*, and the *wrath* of *God* against *Him* untill *Repentance* : said he your *words words were never out of my heart to this present*; and said hee *me much pray to Jesus Christ* : I told him so did many *English*, *French*, and *Dutch*, who had never turned to *God*, nor loved Him : He replyed in broken English : M*e so big naughty Heart, me heart all one stone*! *Savory expressions* using to breath *from compunct and broken Hearts*, and a fence of *inward hardnesse* and *unbrokennesse*. I had many discourses with him in his Life, but this was the summe of our last parting untill our generall meeting:

Now because this is the great Inquiry of all men what *Indians* have been converted? what have the *English* done in those parts? what hopes of the *Indians* receiving the Knowledge of Christ !

And because to this Question, some put

an

To *the Reader.*

an edge from the boast of the Jesuits in *Canada* and *Maryland,* and especially from the wonderfull conversions made by the Spaniards and Portugalls in the *West-Indies,* besides what I have here written, as also, beside what I have observed in the Chapter of their Religion*!* I shall further present you with a briefe Additionall discourse concerning this Great Point, being comfortably perswaded that that Father of Spirits, who was graciously pleased to perswade *Japhet* (the Gentiles) to dwell in the Tents of *Shem* (the *I*ewes) will in his holy season (*I* hope approaching) per-swade, these Gentiles of *America* to partake of the mercies of *Europe,* and then shall bee fulfilled what is written, by the Prophet *Malachi,* from the rising of the Sunne in (*Europe*) to the going down of the same (in *America*) my Name shall great among the Gentiles.) So I desire to hope and pray,

Y̆our unworthy Country-man

Roger Williams.

Directions for the use of the
LANGUAGE.

I. A Dictionary *or* Grammer *way I had consideration of, but purposely avoided, as not so accommodate to the Benefit of all, as I hope this Forme is.*

2. *A* Dialogue *also I had thoughts of, but avoided for brevities sake, and yet (with no small paines) I have so framed every Chapter and the matter of it, as I may call it am Implicite Dialogue.*

3. *It is framed chiefly after the* Narrogánset *Dialect, because most spoken in the Countrey, and yet (with attending to the variation of peoples and Dialects) it will be of great use in all parts of the Countrey.*

4. *Whatever your occasion bee eiiher of Travell, Discourse, Trading &c.*
turne to the Table which will direct you to the Proper Chapter.

5. *Because the Life of all Language is in the Pronuntiation, I have been at the paines and charges to Cause the Accents, Tones or sounds to be affixed, (which some understand, acoording to the* Greeke *Language, Acutes, Graves, Circumflexes) for ex-*
ample,

Directions for the use of the *Language*.

ample, *in the second leafe in the word* Ewò
He: *the sound or Tone must not be put on* E,
but wò *where the grave Accent is*.

In the same leafe, *in the word* Ascowe-
quássin, *the sound must not be on any of the
Syllables, but on* quáss, *where the Acute or
sharp sound is*.

In the same leafe in the word Anspaump-
maûntam, *the sound must not be on any other
syllable but* Maûn, *where the Circumflex or
long sounding Accent is*.

6. *The* English *for every* Indian *word or
phrase stands in a straight line directly against
the* Indian: *yet sometimes there are two words
for the same thing (for their Language is exceeding copious, and they have five or six words
sometimes for one thing) and then the* English
*stands against them both: for example in the
second leafe*,

Cowáunckamish & Cuckquénamish	*I pray your Favour.*

AN
Helpe to the native Language
of that part of *America* called
NEW-ENGLAND.

CHAP. I.
Of *Salutation*.

Observation.

He Natives are of two sorts, (as the English are.) Some more Rude and Clownish, who are not so apt to Salute, but upon *Salutation* resalute lovingly. Others, and the generall, are *sober* and *grave*, and yet chearfull in a meane, and as ready to begin a Salutation as to Resalute, which yet the English generally begin, out of desire to Civilize them.

B   *What*

What cheare Nétop? *is the generall saluta-tion of all* English *toward them,* Nétop *is friend.*

| Netompaûog | *Friends.* |

They are exceedingly delighted with Salutations in their own Language.

Neèn, Keèn, Ewò,	*I, you, he.*
Keèn ka neen	*You and I.*
Asco wequássin	
Asco wequassunnúm-mis	*Goodmorrow.*
Askuttaaquompsìn?	*Hou doe you?*
Asnpaumpmaûntam	*I am very well.*
Taubot paump-maúntaman	*I am glad you are well.*
Cowaúnckamish	*My service to you.*

Observation.

This word upon speciall Salutations they use, and upon some offence conceived by the *Sachim* or Prince against any: I have seen the party reverently doe obeysance, by stroking the Prince upon both his sholders, and using this word,

Cowaúnckamish & Cuckquénamish	*I pray your favour.*
Cowaúnkamuck	*He salutes you.*
Aspaumpmáuntam sachim	*How doth the Prince?*

Aspaum-

Aspaumpmáuntam Commíttamus?	*How doth your Wife?*
Aspaumpmaúntam-wock cummucki-aûg?	*How doth your children?*
Konkeeteâug	*They are well.*
Táu bot ne paump maunthéttit	*I am glad they are well.*
Túnna Cowâum Tuckôteshana	*Whence come you.*
Yò nowaûm	*I came that way.*
Náwwatuck nôteshem	*I came from farre.*
Mattaâsu nóteshem	*I came from hard by.*
Wêtu	*An House.*
Wetuômuck nóte shem	*I came from the house.*
Acâwmuck notéshem	*I came over the water.*
Otàn	*A Towne.*
Otânick notéshem	*I came from the Towne.*

Observation.

In the Narigánset Countrey (which is the chief people in the Land :) a man shall come to many Townes, some bigger, some lesser, it may be a dozen in 20. miles Travell.

Obser-

Observation.

Acawmenóakit *Old England*, which is as much as from the *Land on t'other side:* hardly are they brought to believe that that Water is three thousand English mile over, or thereabouts.

Tunnock kuttòme	*Whither goe you?*
Wékick nittóme	*To the house.*
Nékick	*To my house.*
Kékick	*To your house.*
Tuckowêkin	*Where dwell you?*
Tuckuttîin	*Where keep you?*
Matnowetuómeno	*I have no house.*

Observation.

As commonly a single person hath no house, so after the death of a Husband or Wife, they often break up house, and live here and there a while with Friends, to allay their excessive Sorrowes.

Tou wuttîin?	*Where lives he?*
Awânick ûchick	*Who are these?*
Awaùn ewò?	*Who is that?*
Túnna úmwock?	*Whence come they?*
Tunna Wutshaûock	
Yo nowêkin	*I dwell here.*
Yo ntîin	*I live here.*

Eîu

Eîu *or* Nnîu?	*Is it so?*
Nùx	*Yea.*
Mat nippompitám-men	*I have heard nothing.*
Wésuonck	*A name.*
Tocketussawêitch	*What is your name?*
Taantússawese?	*Doe you aske my name?*
Ntússawese	*I am called, &c.*
Matnowesuónckane	*I have no name.*

Observation.

Obscure and meane persons amongst them have no Names: *Nullius numeri, &c.* as the Lord Jesus foretells his followers, that their Names should be cast out, *Luk. 6. 22.* as not worthy to be named, *&c.* Againe, because they abhorre to name the dead (Death being the King of Terrours to all naturall men: and though the Natives hold the Soule to live ever, yet not holding a Resurrection, they die, and mourn without Hope.) In that respect I say, if any of their *Sáchims* or neighbours die who were of their names, they lay down those Names as dead.

Now ánnehick now-ésuonck	*I have forgot my Name.*

Which is common amongst some of them, this being one Incivilitie amongst the more

rusticall sort, not to call each other by their
Names, but Keen, *You*, Ewò *He*, &c.

Tahéna	*What is his name?*
Tahossowêtam	*What is the name of it?*
Tahéttamen	*What call you this?*
Teáqua	*What is this?*
Yò néepoush	*Stay or stand here.*
Máttapsh	*Sit down.*
Noónshem	
Non ânum	*I cannot.*
Tawhitch kuppee yaúmen	*What come you for?*
Téaqua kunnaúnta men	*What doe you fetch?*
Chenock cuppeeyâu mis?	*When came you?*
Maìsh-kitummâyi	*Iust even now.*
Kitummâyi nippeé-am	*I came just now.*
Yò Committamus?	*Is this your Wife?*
Yo cuppáppoof	*Is this your Child?*
Yò cummúckqua-chucks	*Is this your Son?*
Yò cuttaûnis	*Is this your Daughter?*
Wunnêtu	*It is a fine Child.*
Tawhich neepou-weéye an	*Why stand you?*
Pucqúatchick?	*Without dores.*

Taw-

Tawhítch mat pe ti-teáyean?	*Why come you not in?*

Observ.

In this respect they are remarkably free and courteous, to invite all Strangers in; and if any come to them upon any occasion, they request them to *come in,* if they come not in of themselves.

Awássish	*Warme you.*
Máttapsh yóteg	*Sit by the fire.*
Tocketúnnawem	*What say you?*
Keén nétop?	*Is it you friend.*
Peeyàush nétop	*Come hither friend.*
Pétitees	*Come in.*
Kunnúnni	*Have you seene me?*
Kunnúnnous	*I have seen you.*
Taubot mequaun namêan	*I thank you for your kind remembrance.*
Taûbotneanawáyean	*I thank you.*
Taûbotne aunana-mêan	*I thank you for your love.*

Observ.

I have acknowledged amongst them an heart sensible of kindnesses, and have reaped kindnesse against from many, seaven yeares after, when I my selfe had forgotten, &c hence

B 4 the

the Lord Jesus exhorts his followers to doe
good for evill: for otherwise, sinners will do
good for good, kindnesse for kindnesse, &c.

Cowàmmaunsh	*I love you.*
Cowammaûnuck	*He loves you.*
Cowámmaus	*You are loving.*
Cowâutam?	*Vnderstand you?*
Nowaûtam	*I understand.*
Cowâwtam tawhit-che nippeeyaûmen	*Doe you know why I come.*
Cowannantam	*Have you forgotten?*
Awanagusantowosh	*Speake English.*
Eenàntowash	*Speake Indian.*
Cutehanshishaùmo	*How many were you in Company?*
Kúnnishishem?	*Are you alone?*
Nníshishem	*I am alone.*
Naneeshâumo	*There be 2. of us.*
Nanshwishâwmen	*We are 4.*
Npiuckshâwmen	*We are 10.*
Neesneechecktashaû-men	*We are 20. &c.*
Nquitpausuckowash-âwmen	*We are an 100.*
Comishoonhómmis	*Did you come by boate?*
Kuttiakewushaùmis	*Came you by land?*
Mesh nomishoon hómmin	*I came by boat.*

Mesh

meshntiauké wushem	*I came by land.*
Nippenowàntawem	*I am of another language*
Penowantowawhet-tûock	*They are of a divers language.*
Mat nowawtau hetté mina	*We understand not each other.*
Nummaúchenèm?	*I am sicke.*
Cummaúchenem?	*Are you sicke?*
Tashúckqunne cum mauchenaûmis	*How long have you been sicke?*
Nummauchêmin *or* Ntannetéimmin	*I will be going.*
Saûop Cummauchê-min	*You shall goe to morrow.*
Maúchish *or* ànakish	*Be going.*
Kuttannâwshesh	*Depart.*
Mauchéi *or* ànittui	*He is gone.*
Kautanaûshant	*He being gone.*
Mauchéhettit *or* Kautanawshàwhettit	*When they are gone.*
Kukkowêtous	*I will lodge with you.*
Yò Cówish	*Do lodge here.*
Hawúnshech	*Farewell.*
Chénock wonck cup peeyeâumen?	*When will you be here againe?*
Nétop tattà	*My friend I cannot tell.*

From these courteous *Salutations* Observe in generall: There is a favour of *civility* and
courtesie

courtesie even amongst these wild *Americans*, both amongst *themselves* and towards *strangers*.

   More particular :
   1. *The Courteous* Pagan *shall condemne* Uncourteous Englishmen,
Who live like Foxes, Beares and Wolves,
   Or Lyon in his Den.
   2. *Let none sing* blessings *to their soules,*
      For that they Courteous are:
The wild Barbarians *with no more*
   Then Nature, goe so farre:
   3. *If Natures Sons both* wild *and* tame,
      Humane and Courteous be:
How ill becomes it Sonnes of God
   To want Humanity?

C H A P . II.
Of *Eating* and *Entertainment*.

AScúmetesímmis?	*Have you not yet eaten?*
Matta niccat- tuppúmmin	*I am not hungry.*
Niccàwkatone	*I am thirstie.*
Mannippêno?	*Have you no water?*
Nip, *or* nipéwese	*Give me some water.*
Nàmitch, commete- símmin	*Stay, you must eat first.*
	Teaqua

| Téaquacumméich | *What will you eat?* |
| Nókehick. | *Parch'd meal,* which is |

a readie very wholesome food, which they eate with a little water, hot or cold; I have travelled with neere 200. of them at once, neere 100. miles through the woods, every man carrying a *little Basket* of this at his *back*, and sometimes in a hollow *Leather Girdle* about his middle sufficient for a man three or foure daies:

With this readie provision, and their *Bow* and *Arrowes*, are they ready for *War*, and *travell* at an *houres* warning. With a *spoonfull* of this *meale* and a *spoonfull* of water from the *Brooke*, have I made many a good dinner and supper.

Aupúmmineanash.	*The parch'd corne.*
Aupúminea-naw-saùmp.	*The parc'd meale boild with water at their houses, which is the wholesomest diet they have.*
Msíckquatash.	*Boild corne whole.*
Manusqussêdash.	*Beanes.*
Nasàump.	*A kind of meale pottage, unpartch'd.*

From this the *English* call their *Samp,* which is the *Indian* corne, beaten and boild, and eaten hot or cold with milke or butter, which are

mercies

mercies beyond the *Natives* plaine water, and which is a dish exceeding wholesome for the *English* bodies.

Puttuckqunnége.	*A Cake.*
Puttuckqunnêgunash puttúckqui.	*Cakes or loves round.*
Teâgun kuttie maûnch?	*What shall I dresse for you?*
Assámme.	*Give me to eate.*
Ncàttup.	*I am hungrie.*
Wúnna ncáttup	*I am very hungry.*
Nippaskanaûn tum.	*J am almost starved.*
Pàutous notatàm.	*Give me drinke.*
Sókenish.	*Powre forth.*
Cosaûme sokenúm mis.	*You have powred out too much.*
Wuttàttash.	*Drinke.*
Nquitchetàmmin.	*Let me taste.*
Quítchetash.	*Taste.*
Saúnqui nip?	*Is the water coole?*
Saun kopaûgot.	*Coole water.*
Chowhêsu	*It is warme,*
Aquie wuttàttash.	*Doe not drinke.*
Aquie waúmatous.	*Doe not drinke all.*
Necáwni mèich teàqua.	*First eat something:*
Tawhitch mat me chóan.	*Why eat you not?*

Wussaúme

Wussaúme kusópira.	*It is too hot.*
Teâguun numméitch	*What shall I eate?*
Mateàgkeesitáuano?	*Is there nothing ready boyld?*
Mateàg mécho ewò	*He eats nothing.*
Cotchikésu assamme.	*Cut me a piece.*
Cotchekúnnemi wee yoùs.	*Cut me some meat.*
Metesíttuck.	*Let us goe eate.*
Pautiínnea méchimucks.	*Bring hither some victualls.*
Numwàutous.	*Fill the dish.*
Mihtukmécha kick.	*Tree-eaters.* A people so called (living be-

tween three and foure hundred miles West in-
to the land) from their eating only *Mihtúch-quash*, that is, Trees: They are *Men-eaters*,
they set no corne, but live on the *bark* of *Chesnut* and *Walnut*, and other fine trees: They dry
and eat this *bark* with the fat of Beasts, and
somtimes of men: This people are the *terrour*
of the neighbour *Natives*; and yet these *Rebells*, the Sonne of God may in time subdue.

Mauchepweéean.	*After I have eaten.*
Maúchepwucks.	*After meales.*
Maúchepwut.	*When he hath eaten.*
Paúshaqua maúchepwut.	*After dinner.*
	Wàyyeyant

Wàyyeyant maúche-pwut.	*After supper.*
Nquittmaûntash.	*Smell.*
Weetimóquat.	*It smells sweet.*
Machemóqut.	*It stinks.*
Weékan.	*It is sweet.*
Machíppiquat.	*It is sowre.*
Aúwusse weékan.	*It is sweeter.*
Askùn.	*It is raw.*
Noónat.	*Not enough.*
Wusàume wékissu.	*Too much either boyled or rosted.*
Waûmet Taûbi.	*It is enough.*
Wuttattumútta.	*Let us drinke.*
Neesneechàhettit taúbi.	*Enough for twentie men.*
Mattacuckquàw.	*A Cooke.*
Mattacúcquass.	*Cooke or dresse.*
Matcuttàssamíin?	*Will you not give me to eate?*
Keen méitch.	*I pray eate.*

They generally all take *Tobacco;* and it is commonly the only plant which men labour in; the women managing all the rest: they say they take *Tobacco* for two causes; first, against the rheume, which cavseth the tooth-ake, which they are impatient of: secondly, to revive and refresh them, they drinking no-thing but water.   Squttame.

Squuttame.	*Give me your pipe.*
Petasínna, *or,* Wuttàmmasin.	*Give mee some Tabacco.*
Ncattaûntum, *or,* Ncàttiteam.	*I long for that.*
Màuchinaash nowépiteass.	*My teeth are naught.*
Nummashackqune aûmen.	*Wee are in a dearth.*
Mashackquineâug.	*We have no food.*
Aúcuck.	*A Kettle.*
Míshquockuk.	*A red Copper Kettle*
Nétopkuttàssammish.	*Friend, I have brought you this.*
Quàmphash quamphomïinea.	*Take up for me out of the pot.*
Eíppoquat.	*It is sweet.*
Teàqua aspúckquat?	*What doth it taste of?*
Nowétipo.	*I like this.*
Wenómeneash.	*Grapes or Raysins.*
Waweécocks.	*Figs, or some strange sweet meat.*
Nemaúanash.	*Provision for the way.*
Nemauanínnuit.	*A snapsacke.*
Tackhúmmin.	*To grind corne.*
Tackhumíinnea.	*Beat me parch'd meale.*
Pishquéhick.	*Vnparch'd meale.*
Nummaùchip nup mauchepúmmin.	*We have eaten all.*

Cow-

Cowàump?	*Have you enough?*
Nowâump.	I *have enough.*
Mohowaúgsuck, *or,* Mauquàuog, *from* móho *to eate.*	*The* Canibals, *or,* Men-eaters, *up into the west, two, three or foure hundred miles from us.*
Cummóhucquock.	*They will eate you.*

Whomsoever commeth in when they are eating, they offer them to eat of that which they have, though but little enough prepar'd for themselves. If any provision of *fish* or *flesh* come in, they make their neighbours partakers with them.

If any stranger come in, they presently give him to eate of what they have; many a time, and at all times of the night (as I have fallen in travell upon their houses) when nothing hath been ready, have themselves and their wives, risen to prepare me some refreshing.

The observation generall from their eating, &c.

It is a strange *truth*, that a man shall generally finde more free entertainment and refreshing amongst these *Barbarians*, then amongst thousands that call themselves *Christians*.

more

More particular:

1 *Course* bread *and* water's *most their fare;*
  O Englands *diet fine;*
Thy cup *runs ore with plenteous store*
  Of wholesome beare *and* wine.

2 *Sometimes* God *gives them* Fish *or* Flesh,
  Yet they're content *without;*
And what comes in, they part *to* friends
  and strangers *round about.*

3 *Gods* providence *is rich to his,*
  Let none distrustfull *be;*
In wildernesse, *in great* distresse,
  These Ravens *have fed me.*

CHAP. III.

Concerning Sleepe *and* Lodging.

NSowwushkâwmen	*I am weary.*
Nkàtaquaum.	*I am sleepie.*
Kukkovetoùs.	*Shall I lodge here?*
Yo nickowémen?	*Shall I sleepe here?*
Kukkowéti.	*Will you sleepe here?*
Wunnégin, cówish.	*Welcome, sleepe here.*
Nummouaquômen.	*I will lodge abroad.*

C   Puck-

Puckquátchick nick-ouêmen. | *I will sleepe without the the doores*, Which I

have knowne them contentedly doe, by a fire under a tree, when sometimes some *English* have (for want of familiaritie and language with them) been fearefull to entertaine them.

In Summer-time I have knowne them lye abroad often themselves, to make roome for strangers, *English,* or others.

Mouaquómitea.	*Let us lye abroad.*
Cowwêtuck.	*Let us sleepe.*
Kukkóuene?	*Sleepe you?*
Cowwêke.	*Sleepe, sleepe.*
Cowwêwi.	*He is asleepe.*
Cowwêwock.	*They sleepe.*
Askukkówene?	*Sleepe you yet?*
Takitíppocat.	*It is a cold night.*
Wekitíppocat.	*It is a warme night.*
Wauwháutowaw ánawat & Wawhautowâvog.	*Ther is an alarme*, or, *there is a great shouting*: Howling and

shouting is their Alarme; they having no Drums nor Trumpets: but whether an enemie approach, or fire breake out, this Alarme passeth from house to house; yea, commonly, if any *English* or *Dutch* come amongst them, they give notice of strangers by this signe; yet I have knowne them buy and use a *Dutch* Trumpet,

Trumpet, and knowne a *Native* make a good
Drum in imitation of the *English*.

Matànnauke, *or* Mat-tannaukanash	*A finer sort of mats to sleep on.*
Mask tuash	*Straw to ly on.*
Wuddtúckqunash ponamâuta	*Let us lay on wood.*

This they doe plentifully when they lie
down to sleep winter and summer, abundance
they have and abundance they lay on: their
Fire is instead of our bedcloaths. And so,
themselves and any that have occasion to
lodge with them, must be content to turne
often to the Fire if the night be cold, and they
who first wake must repaire the Fire.

Mauataúnamoke	*Mend the fire.*
Mauataunamútta	*Let us mend the fire.*
Tokêtuck	*Let us wake.*
As kuttokémis	*Are you not awake yet*
Tokish Tokeke	*Wake wake*
Tókinish	*Wake him.*
Kitumyái tokéan	*As soone as I wake.*
Ntunnaquômen	*I have had a good dream*
Nummattaquômen	*I have had a bad dream.*

When they have a bad Dreame, which they
conceive to be a threatning from God, they
fall to prayer at all times of the night, especially early before day: So *Davids* zealous heart

to the true and living God: *At midnight will
I rise,* &c. *I prevented the dawning of the day,*
&c. Psal. 119. &c.

Wunnakukkússa quaùm	*You sleep much.*
Peeyaûntam	*He prayes.*
Peeyâuntamwock	*They pray.*
Túnna kukkowémis	*Where slept you?*
Awaun wéick kuk- kouémis	*At whose house did you sleep?*

    I once travailed to an Iland of the wildest in
our parts, where in the night an Indian (as he
said) had a vision or dream of the Sun (whom
they worship for a God) darting a Beame
into his Breast which he conceived to be the
Messenger of his Death: this poore Native
call'd his Friends and neighbours and prepared some little refreshing for them, but himselfe was kept waking and Fasting in great
Humiliations and Invocations for 10. dayes
and nights: I was alone (having travailed from
my Barke, the wind being contrary) and little
could I speake to them to their understand-
ings especially because of the change of their
Dialect, or manner of Speech from our neighbours: yet so much (through the help of God)
I did speake, of the *True* and *living only Wise
God*, of the Creation: of Man, and his *fall*
from

from God, &c. that at parting many burst
forth, *Oh when will you come againe, to bring
us some more newes of this God?*

From their Sleeping: The Observation generall.

Sweet rest is not confind to soft Beds, for,
not only God gives his beloved sleep on hard
lodgings: but also Nature and Custome gives
sound sleep to these Americans on the Earth,
on a Boord or Mat. Yet how is *Europe* bound
to God for better lodging, *&c.*

More particular.

1. *God gives them sleep on Ground, on Straw,*
    on Sedgie Mats or Boord:
When English softest Beds of Downe,
    sometimes no sleep affoord.

2. *J have knowne them leave their House and*
        Mat
    to lodge a Friend or stranger,
When Jewes and Christians oft have sent
    Christ Jesus *to the Manger.*

3. *'Fore day they invocate their Gods,*
    though Many, False and New:
O how should that God worshipt be,
    who is but One and True?

Chap. IIII.

Of *their* Names.

NQuít	*One*
Neèsse	2.
Nìsh	3.
Yòh	4.
Napànna	5.
Qútta	6.
énada	7.
Shwósuck	8.
Paskúgit	9.
Piùck	10.
Piuck nabna quit	11.
Piucknab nèese	12,
Piucknab nìsh	13,
Piucknab yòh	14,
Piucknab napànna	15,
Piucknab naqútta	16;
Piucknab énada	17,
Piuck nabna shwó-suck	18,
Piucknab napas-kúgit	19,
Neesneéchick	20,

Nees-

Neesneĕchick nab na- quìt, &c.	21,
Shwínckeck	30,&c.
Swíncheck nab na- quìt, &c.	31,&c.
Yowínicheck	40.
Yówinicheck nabna qìt, &c.	41,&c.
Napannetashincheck	50,
Napannetashinchek nabna quit	51,&c.
Quttatashìncheck	60,
Quttatashincheck nab na quìt	61,&c.
Enadatashìncheck	70,
Enadatashincheck nabna quìt	71,&c.
Swoasuck ta shin check	80,
Shwoasuck ta shin- check nebna quìt	81,&c.
Paskugit tashìn- check, &c.	90,
Paskugit tashin check nabna quìt, &c.	91,&c.
Nquit pâwsuck	100.
Nees pâwsuck	200.
Shweepâwsuck	300.

B 4   Yówe

Yówe pâwsuck	400,
Napannetashe pâw-suck	500,
Qúttatashe pâwsuck	600,
Enadatashepâwsuck	700,
Shoasucktashe pâw-suck	800,
Paskugit tashepâw-suck	900,
Nquittemittànnug	1000,
Neese mittànnug	2000,
Nishwe mittànnug	3000,
Yowe mittànnug	4000,
Napannetaíhemit tànnug	5000,
Quttàtashe mit tàn-nug	6000
Enadatashemit tàn-nug	7000,
Shoasuck ta she mit-tánnug	8000,
Paskugittashemit tánnug	9000,
Piuckque mittánnug	10000,
Neesneecheck tashe mittânnug	20000,
Shwinchecktashe mittánnug	30000,

Yow-

Yowincheck tashe-mittânnug	40000,
Napannetashincheck tashemittánnug	50000.
Quttatashincheck ta-shemittànnug	60000.
Enadatashincheck tashe mittánnuck	70000.
Shoasuck tashincheck tashe mittannug	80000.
Pàskugit tashincheck tashe mittànnug	90000.
Nquit pausuckóemit tànnug, *&c.*	100000.

Having no Letters nor Arts, 'tis admirable how quick they are in casting up great numbers, with the helpe of graines of Corne, instead of *Europes* pens or counters.

Numbers of the masculine gender.

Pâwsuck	1.	
Neéswock	2.	Skeetomp *a Man.*
Shúog	3.	
Yówock	4.	{ Skeetom
Napannetasúog	5. *as,*	{ Paúog,
Quttasúog	6.	{ *Men.*
Enada tasúog	7.	
Shoasuck tasúog	8.	

Pas-

Paskugit tasúog	9.
Piucksúog	10.
Piucksúog nabna- quìt	11.

Of the *Feminine* Gender.

Pâwsuck	1		
Neénash	2		
Swínash	3		
Yowúnnash	4		Wauchò
Napannetashínash	5		*Hill.*
Quttatashínash	6	*as,*	Wauchóash
Enadtashínash	7		*Hills.*
Shoasucktashínash	8		
Paskugittashínash	9		
Piúckquatash	10		
Piúckquatash nabna- quìt	11		

From their Numbers, *Observation* Generall.

Let it be considered, whether *Tradition* of ancient *Forefathers*, or *Nature* hath taught them *Europes Arithmaticke*.

More particular :

1 *Their* Braines *are quick, their* hands,
  Their feet, *their* tongues, *their* eyes:

God

God may fit objects *in his time,*
  To those quicke faculties.
2 Objects *of higher nature make them tell,*
  The holy number *of his Sons* Gospel:
Make them and us to tell *what* told *may be*;
  But stand amazed *at* Eternitie.

Chap. V.

Of their relations *of* consanguinitie *and*
affinitie, *or,* Blood *and* Marriage.

NNìn-nnínnuog, & Skeétomp-aûog	*Man-men*
Squàws-suck	*Woman-women.*
Kichize, &	*An old man,*
Kichîzuck	*Old men*
Hômes, &	*An old man,*
Hômesuck	*Old men.*
Kutchínnu	*A middle-aged-man.*
Kutchinnuwock.	*Middle-aged-men.*
Wuskeène	*A youth,*
Wuskeeneésuck.	*Youths.*
Wénise &	*An old woman,*
Wenîsuck	*Old women.*
Mattaûntum	*Very old and decrepit.*

Wásick

Wásick	*An Husband.*
Weéwo, &	*A Wife.*
Mittúmmus, &	
Wullógana	
Nowéewo,	*My Wife.*
Nummíttamus, &c.	
Osh.	*A Father.*
Nòsh	*My father.*
Còsh	*Your father.*
Cuttòso?	*Have you a father?*
Okásu, &	*A mother.*
Wítchwhaw	
Nókace, nítchwhaw	*My mother*
Wússese	*An Vnckle.*
Nissesè	*My Vnckle.*
Papoòs,	*A childe.*
Nippápoos, &	*My childe.*
Nummúckiese	
Nummúckquáchucks	*My sonne.*
Nittaûnis	*My daughter.*
Non ânese	*A sucking child.*
Muck quachuckquê- mese	*A little boy.*
Squásese	*A little girle.*
Weémat.	*A brother.*

They hold the band of brother-hood so deare, that when one had commited a mur- ther and fled, they executed his brother; and
'tis

'tis common for a brother to pay the debt of
a brother deceased.

Neémat	*My brother.*
Wéticks, &	*A sister.*
Weésummis	
Wematíttuock	*They are brothers.*
Cutchashematítin?	*How many brothers have you?*
Natòncks	*My cousin.*
Kattòncks	*Your cousin.*
Watòncks	*A cousin.*
Nullóquaso	*My ward or pupill.*
Wattonksíttuock	*They are cousins.*
Kíhtuckquaw	*A virgin marriageable.*

Their Virgins are distinguished by a bash-
full falling downe of their haire over their
eyes.

Towiúwock	*Fatherlesse children.*

There are no beggars amongst them, nor fa-
therlesse children unprovided for.

Tackqíuwock	*Twins.*

Their *affections*, especially to their children,
are very strong; so that I have knowne a *Father* take so grievously the losse of his *childe*,
that hee hath cut and stobd himselfe with
griefe and *rage*.

This extreme *affection*, together with want
of *learning*, makes ther children sawcie, bold,
and undutifull.   I

I once came into a *house,* and requested some *water* to drinke; the *father* bid his sonne (of some 8.yeeres of age) to fetch some *water:* the *boy* refused, and would not stir; I told the *father,* that I would correct my *child,* if he should so disobey me, &c. Upon this the *father* took up a sticke, th*e boy* another, and flew at his *father;* upon my perswasion, the poor *father* made him smart a little, threw down his stick, and run for *water,* and the *father* confessed the benefit of *correction,* and the evill of their too indulgent *affections.*

From their ⎫
Relations ⎬ *Observation generall.*

In the *ruines* of depraved *mankinde,* are yet to be founde *Natures distinctions,* and *Nature's affections.*

More particular :
The Pagans *wild confesse the* bonds
    Of married chastitie:
How vild are Nicolâitans *that hold*
    Of Wives *communitie?*
How kindly flames of nature *burne*
    In wild humanitie:
Naturall affections *who wants, is sure*
    Far from Christianity.

Best

Best nature's vaine, he's blest that's made
  A new and rich partaker
Of divine Nature of his God,
  And blest eternall Maker.

CHAP. VI.

Of the Family and businesse of the House.

VVEtu	*An House.*
Wetuómuck	*At home.*
Nékick	*My house.*
Kékick	*Your house.*
Wk ick	*At his house.*
Nickquénum.	*I am going home :*

Which is a solemne word amongst them; and no man wil offer any hinderance to him, who after some absence is going to visit his Family, and useth this word *Nicquénum* (confessing the sweetnesse even of these short temporall homes.)

Puttuckakàun	*A round house.*
Puttcukakâunese	*A little round house.*
Wetuomémese	*A little house;* which

their women and maids live apart in, four,

five

five, or six dayes, in the time of their moneth-
ly sicknesse, which custome in all parts of the
Countrey they strictly observe, and no *Male*
may come into that house.

Neés quttow	*A longer house with two fires.*
Shwíshcuttow	*With three fires.*
Abockquósinash	*The mats of the house.*
Wuttapuíssuck	*The long poles,* which

commonly men get and fix, and then the women cover the house with mats, and line
them with embroydered mats which the women make, and call them *Mannotaúbana,* or
Hangings, which amongst them make as faire
a show as Hangings with us.

Nòte, *or* Yòte	
Chíckot *&*	*Fire.*
Squtta :	
Notáwese *&* chickau- táwese	*A little fire.*
Púck	*Smoke.*
Puckíssu	*Smokie*
Nippúckis	*Smoke troubleth me.*
Wuchickapêuck	*Burching barke,* and

Chesnut barke which they dresse finely, and
make a Summer-covering for their houses.

Cuppoquiíttemin.	*I will divide house with you,* or *dwell with you.*

Two

Two Families will live comfortably and lovingly in a little round house of some fourteen or sixteen foot over, and so more and more families in proportion.

Núckquiquatch	*I am cold.*
Nuckqusquatchímin	
Potouwássiteuck	*Let us make a fire.*
Wúdtuckqun	*A piece of wood.*
Wudtúckquanash	*Lay on wood.*
Ponamâuta	
Pawacómwushesh	*Cut some wood.*
Maumashinnaunam aûta	*Let us make a good fire.*
Npaacómwushem	*I will cut wood.*
Aséneshesh	*Fetch some small sticks.*
Wònck, &	*More.*
Wónkatack	
Wonckataganash nàus	*Fetch some more*
Netashin & newuchá- shinea,	*There is no more.*
Wequanántash	*A light fire.*
Wequanantig	*A Candle,* or *Light.*
Wequanantíganash	*Candles.*
Wékinan	*A light fire.*
Awâuo?	*Who is at home?*
Mat Awawanúnno	*There is no body.*
Unháppo Kòsh	*Is your father at home?*

D   Túckiu

Túckiu Sáchim	*Where is the Sachim?*
Mat-apeù	*He is not at home*
Peyàu	*He is come.*
Wéche-peyàu-keé mat	*Your brother is come with him.*
Pótawash	*Make a fire.*
Potâuntash	*Blowe the fire.*
Peeyâuog	*They are come*
Wâme, paúshe	*All-some.*
Tawhìtch mat peyá-yean	*Why came, or, came you not.*
Mesh noónshem pee-yaùn?*	*I could not come.*
Mocenanippeéam	*I will come by and by.*
Aspeyàu, asquàm	*He is not come yet.*
Yò aútant mèsh nip-peéam	*I was here the Sunne so high.* And then they

point with the hand to the Sunne, by whose highth they keepe account of the day, and by the Moone and Stars by night, as wee doe by clocks and dialls, &c.

Wúskont peyâuog	*They will come.*
Teáqua naúntick ewò	*What comes hee for?*
Yo áppitch ewò	*Let him sit there.*
Unhappò kòsh	*Is your father at home?*
Unnàugh	*He is there.*
Npépeyup náwwot	*I have long been here.*

Tawìtch

Tawhìtch peyáuyean	*Why doe you come?*
Téaguun kunnaúntamun?	*What come you for?*
Awàun ewò?	*Who is that?*
Nowéchiume	*He is my servant.*
Wécum, nàus	*Call fetch.*
Petiteaûta	*Let us goe in.*
Noonapúmmin autashéhettit	*There is not roome for so many.*
Taubapímmin	*Roome enough.*
Noónat	*Not enough.*
Asquam	*Not yet.*
Náim, námitch	*By and by.*
Mòce, unuckquaquêse	*Instantly.*
Máish, kituminay	*Iust, even now.*
Túckiu, tíyu	*Where.*
Kukkekuttokâwmen	*Would you speake with him?*
Nùx	*Yea.*
Wuttammâun tam	*He is busie.*
Nétop notammâun tam	*Friend, I am busie.*
Cotammâuntam	*Are you busie?*
Cotámmish	*I hinder you.*
Cotammúmme ⎱ Cotamme ⎰	*You trouble me.*

Obs. They

Obs. They are as full of businesse, and as impatient of hinderance (in their kind) as any Merchant in *Europe.*

Nqussûtam	*I am removing.*
Notámmehick ewò	*He hinders me.*
Maumachíuash	*Goods.*
Aúquiegs	*Housholdstuffe.*
Tuckíiuash	*Where be they?*
Wenawwêtu	*Rich.*
Machêtu	*Poore.*
Wenawetuónckon	*Wealth.*
Kúphash	*Shut the doore.*
Kuphómmin	*To shut the doore.*
Yeaùsh	*Shut doore after you.*

Obs. Commonly they never shut their doores, day nor night; and 'tis rare that any hurt is done.

Wunêgin	*Well, or good.*
Machit	*Naught, or evill.*
Cowaûtam?	*Do you understand?*
Macháug	*No, or not.*
Wunnáug	*A Tray.*
Wunnauganash	*Trayes.*
Kunàm	*A Spoone.*
Kunnamâuog	*Spoones.*

Obs. In steed of shelves, they have severall baskets, wherein they put all their housholdstuffe

stuffe: they have some great bags or sacks made of *Hempe*, which will hold five or sixe bushells.

Táckunck, *or,* ⎫ Wéskhunck. ⎭	| *Their pounding Mor-* *ter.*

Obs. Their women constantly beat all their corne with hand: they plant it, dresse it, gather it, barne it, beat it, and take as much paines as any people in the world, which labour is questionlesse one cause of their extraordinary ease of childbirth.

Wunnauganémese	*A little Tray.*
Téaqua cunnatinne	*What doe you looke for?*
Natínnehas	*Search.*
Kekíneas	*See here.*
Machàge cunna mi- teôuwin?	*Doe you find nothing.*
Wónckatack	*Another.*
Tunnati	*Where.*
Ntauhaunanatinne- hómmin	*I cannot looke or* *search.*
Ntauhaunanamiteoû- win	*I cannot find.*
Wíaseck Eiássunck Mocôtick Punnêtunck Chaúqock.	*A Knife.*

D 3   *Obs.* Whence

Obs. Whence they call *English-men* Cháu-
quaquock, that is, *Knive-men*, stone formerly
being to them in stead of *Knives, Awle-blades,
Hatchets* and *Howes.*

Namacówhe	*Lend me your Knife.*
Cówíaseck	
Wonck Commêsim?	*Wil you give it me again?*
Mátta nowáuwone	*I knew nothing.*
Matta nowáhea	
Mat meshnowáhea	*I was innocent.*
Paútous, Pautâuog	*Bring hither.*
Maúchatous	*Carry this.*
Niâutash, &	
Wéawhush.	*Take it on your backe.*

Obs. It is almost incredible what burthens
the poore women carry of *Corne*, of *Fish*, of
Beanes, of *Mats*, and a childe besides.

Awâùn	*There is some body.*
Kekíneas	*Goe and see.*
Squauntâumuck	*At the doore.*
Awâun keèn?	*Who are you?*
Keèn nétop	*Is it you.*
Pauquanamíinnea	*Open me the doore.*

Obs. Most commonly their houses are o-
pen, their doore is a hanging *Mat*, which being lift up, falls downe of it selfe; yet many of
them get *English* boards and nailes, and make
artificiall doores and bolts themselves, and
others

others make slighter doores of *Burch* or *Chesnut* barke, which they make fast with a cord in the night time, or when they go out of town, and then the last (that makes fast) goes out at the Chimney which is a large opening in the middle of their house, called:

Wunnauchicomock,	*A Chimney.*
Anúnema	*Helpe me.*
Neenkuttánnŭmous.	*I will helpe you.*
Kuttánnummi?	*Will you helpe me?*
Shookekíneas	*Behold here.*
Nummouekékineam	*I come to see.*
Tou autèg	*Know you where it lies?*
Tou núckquaque	*How much?*
Yo naumwâuteg	*Thus full.*
Aquíe	*Leave off, or doe not.*
Waskéche	*On the top.*
Náumatuck	*In the bottome.*
Aûqunnish	*Let goe.*
Aukeeaseiu	*Downewards.*
Keesuckgíu	*Vpwards.*
Aumàunsh	
Ausàuonsh	*Take away.*
Aumáunamòke.	
Nanóuwetea	*A Nurse,* or *Keeper.*
Naunóuwheant	
Nanowwúnemum	*I looke to,* or *keepe.*

Obs. They

Obs. They nurse all their childrem themselves; yet, if she be an high or rich woman,
she maintaines a Nurse to tend the childe.

Wauchàunama	*Keep this for me.*
Cuttatashiínnas	*Lay these up for me.*

Obs. Many of them begin to be furnished
with *English* Chests; others, when they goe
forth of towne, bring their goods (if they live
neere) to the *English* to keepe for them, and
their money they hang it about their necks,
or lay it under their head when they sleepe.

Peewâuqun	*Have a care.*
N nowauchâunum	*I will have a care.*
Kuttaskwhè	*Stay for me.*
Kúttasha, &	
Cowauchâunum?	*Have you this or that?*
Pókesha, &	
Pokesháwwa.	*It is broke.*
Mat Coanichégane	*Have you no hands?*
Tawhìtch?	*Why aske you?*
Nóonshem Pawtuck-	*I cannot reach.*
quámmin.	
Aquie Pokesháttous.	*Doe not breake.*
Pokesháttouwin.	*To breake.*
Assótu, &	
Assóko.	*A foole.*

Obs. They have also amongst them naturall
foole*s*, either so borne, or accidentally deprived
of reason.   Aquie

Aquie assókish	*Be not foolish.*
Awânick	*Some come.*
Niáutamwock	*They are loden.*
Pauchewannâuog	
Máttapeu &	*A woman keeping alone*
Qushenawsui	*in her monethly sick-*
	nesse.
Moce ntúnnan	*I will tell him by and by.*
Cowequetúmmous	*I pray or intreat you.*
Wunniteóuin	*To mend any thing.*
Wúnniteous, or,	*Mend this,*
Wússiteous.	*Mend this.*
Wúskont noche-	*I shall be chidden.*
múckqun.	
Nickúmmat	*Easie.*
Siúckat	*Hard.*
Cummequâwname?	*Do you remember me?*
Mequaunamíinnea	*Remember me.*
Puckqúatchick	*Without doores.*
Nissawhócunck ewò	*He puts me out of doores.*
Kussawhóki?	*Doe you put mee out of*
	doores?
Kussawhocowóog.	*Put them forth.*
Tawhítch kussàwho-	*Why doe you put mee*
kiêan?	*ont?*
Sáwwhush,	*Goe forth.*
Sawhèke	
Wussauhemútta	*Let us goe forth.*
	Matta

Matta nickquéhick	*I want it not.*
Machagè nickquehic-kômina.	*I want nothing.*

Ob. Many of them naturally Princes, or else industrious persons, are rich and the poore amongst them will say, they want nothing.

Páwsawash.	*Drie or ayre this.*
Pawsunnúmmin.	*To drie this or that.*
Cuppausummúnnash	*Drie these things.*
Apissumma.	*Warme this for me.*
Paucótche	*Already.*
Cutsshitteoùs	*Wash this.*
Tatágganish	*Shake this.*
Napònsh	*Lay downe.*
Wuchè machaùg	*About nothing.*
Puppucksháckhege	*A Box.*
Paupaqúonteg	*A Key.*
Mowáshuck	*Iron.*
Wâuki.	*Crooked.*
Saûmpi	*Strait.*
Aumpaniímmin	*To undoe a knot.*
Aúmpanish	*Vntie this.*
Paushinúmmin	*To divide into two.*
Pepênash	*Take your choyce.*
Nawwuttùnsh Pawtáwtees	*Throw hither.*
Negáutowash	*Send for him.*
Negauchhúwash	*Send this to him.*

Nnegáu-

Nnegâuchemish	*Hee sends to mee.*
Nowwêta	*No matter.*
Mâuo.	*To cry and bewaile;*

Which bewailing is very solemne amongst them morning and evening and sometimes in the night they bewaile their lost husbands, wives, childreu, brethren or sisters &c. Sometimes a quarter, halfe, yea, a whole yeere, and longer, if it be for a great Prince.

In this time (unlesse a dispensation be given) they count it a prophane thing either to play (as they much use to doe) or to paint themselves, for beauty, but for mourning; or to be angry, and fall out with any, &c.

Machemóqut	*It stincks.*
Machemóqussu	*A vile or stinking person.*
Wúnníckshaas	*Mingled.*
Wúnnickshan	*To mingle.*
Nésick & nashóqua.	*A Combe.*
Tetúpsha	*To fall downe.*
Ntetúpshem	*I fall downe.*
Tou anúckquaque?	*How big?*
Wunnáshpishan	*To snatch away.*
Tawhìtch wunnash-pisháyean	*Why snach you?*
Wuttùsh	*Hitherward, & give me.*
Enèick, *or,* áwwusse	*Further.*
Nneickomásu, & aw-wassése.	*A little further.*

Wut-

Wuttushenaquáish	*Looke hither.*
Yo anaquáyean	*Looke about.*
Máuks máugoke	*Give this.*
Yo comméish	*I will give you this.*
Qussúcqun-náukon	*Heavie, light.*
Kuckqússaqun	*You are heavie.*
Kunnàuki	*You are light.*
Nickáttash, *singular.*	*Leave, or depart.*
Nickáttammoke, *plur.*	
Nickattamútta.	*Let us depart.*
Yówa.	*Thus.*
Ntowwaukâumen.	*I use is.*
Awawkáwnì.	*It is used.*
Yo awáutees.	*Vse this.*
Yo wéque.	*Thus farre.*
Yo meshnowékeshem	*I went thus farre.*
Ayátche, &	*as* { *Often.*
Cónkitchea.	
Ayatche nippéeam.	*I am often here.*
Pakêtash.	*Fling it away.*
Npaketamúnnash.	*I will cast him away.*
Wuttámmasim.	*Give me* Tobaco.
Mat nowewuttámmo	*I take none.*

Obs. Which some doe not, but they are rare Birds; for generally all the men throughout the Countrey have a *Tobacco-bag*, with a *pipe* in it, hanging at their back: sometimes they make such great *pipes*, both of *wood* and *stone*, that

that they are two foot long, with men or beasts carved so big or massie, that a man may be hurt mortally by one of them; but these comonly come from the *Mauquáuwogs,* or the *Men eaters,* three or foure hundred miles from us: They have an excellent Art to cast our *Pewter* and *Brasse* into very neate and artificiall *Pipes:* They take their *Wuttam-* mâuog (tkat is, a weake *Tobacco*) which the men plant themselves, very frequently; yet I never see any take so excessively, as I have seene men in *Europe;* and yet excesse were more tolerable in them, because they want the refreshing of *Beare* and *Wine,* which God hath vouchsafed *Europe.*

Wuttámmagon.	*A Pipe.*
Hopuònck.	*A Pipe.*
Chicks.	*A Cocke,* or *Hen* : A

name taken from the *English* Chicke, because they have no Hens before the *English* came.

Chícks ánawat.	*The Cocke crowes.*
Neesquttónckqussu.	*A babler,* or *prater.*
Cunneesquttonck-	*You prate.*
qussímmin.	

Obs. Which they figuratively transferre from the frequent troublesome clamour of a Cocke.

Nanóta-

Nanótateem.	*I keepe house alone.*
Aquìe kuttúnnan.	*Doe not tell.*
Aquìe mooshkishát-tous.	*Doe not disclose.*
Teàg yo augwháttick?	*What hangs there?*
Yo augwháttous.	*Hang it there.*
Pemisquâi.	*Crooked,* or *winding.*
Penâyi.	*Crooked.*
Nqussútam.	*I remove house:* Which

they doe upon these occasions: From thick
warme vallies, where they winter, they remove a little neerer to their Summer fields;
when 'tis warme Spring, then they remove to
their fields where they plant Corne.

In middle of Summer, because of the abundance of Fleas, which the dust of the house
breeds, they will flie and remove on a sudden
from one part of their field to a fresh place:
And sometimes having fields a mile or two,
or many miles asunder, when the worke of
one field is over, they remove house to the
other: If death fall in amongst them, they
presently remove to a fresh place: If an enemie approach, they remove into a Thicket, or
Swampe, unlesse they have some Fort to remove unto.

Sometimes they remove to a hunting house
in the end of the yeere, and forsake it not untill

till Snow lie thick, and then will travel home, men, women and children, thorow the snow, thirtie, yea, fiftie or sixtie miles; but their great remove is from their Summer fields to warme and thicke woodie bottomes where they winter: They are quicke; in halfe a day, yea, sometimes at few houres warning to be gone and the house up elsewhere; especially, if they have stakes readie pitcht for their *Mats.*

I once in travell lodged at a house, at which in my returne I hoped to hàve lodged againe there the next night, but the house was gone in that interim, and I was glad to lodge under a tree:

The men make the poles or stakes, but the women make and set up take downe, order, and carry the *Mats* and housholdstuffe.

Observation in generall.

The sociablenesse of the nature of man appeares in the wildest of them, who love societie; Families, cohabitation, and consociation of houses and townes together.

More

More particular:

1   *How busie are the sonnes of men?*
       How full their heads and hands?
   What noyse and tumults in our owne,
       And eke in Pagan *lands?*

2   *Yet I have found lesse noyse, more peace*
       In wilde America,
   Where women quickly build the house,
       And quickly move away.
   English *and* Indians *busie are,*
       In parts of their abode:
   Yet both stand idle, *till God's call*
       Set them to worke for God.

                              Mat. 20.7.

Chap. VII.

Of *their Persons* and *parts of body.*

UPpaquóntup.	*The head.*
Nuppaquóntup.	*My head.*
Wésheck.	*The hayre.*
Wuchechepúnnock.	*A great bunch of hayre bound up behind.*
Múppacuck.	*A long locke.*

                              Obs Yet

Obs. Yet some cut their haire round, and some as low and as short as the sober *English*; yet I never saw any so to forget nature it selfe in such excessive length and monstrous fashion, as to the shame of the *English* Nation, I now (with griefe) see my Countrey-men in *England* are degenerated unto.

Wuttip. | *The braine.*

Ob. In the braine their opinion is, that the soule (of which we shall speake in the Chapter of *Religion*) keeps her chiefe seat and residence:

For the temper of the braine in quick apprehensions and accurate judgements (to say no more) the most high and soveraign God and Creator, hath not made them inferiour to *Europeans.*

The *Mauquaûogs,* or *Men-eaters,* that live two or three miles West from us, make a delicious monstrous dish of the head and brains of their enemies; which yet is no barre (when the time shall approach) against Gods call, and their repentance, and (who knowes but) a greater love to the Lord Jesus? great sinners forgiven love much.

Mscáttuck.	*The fore-head.*
Wuskeésuck-quash.	*Eye, or eyes.*

Tiyùsh kusskeésuck-
    quash?
	Can you not see, or *where
	    are your eyes?*

F   Wuchaûn

Wuchaûn.	*The nostrills.*
Wuttóvwog, guàsh.	*Eare, eares.*
Wuttòne.	*The mouth.*
Wéenat.	*The tongue.*
Wépit-teash.	*Tooth, teeth.*
Pummaumpiteùnck.	*The tooth-ake.*

Obs. Which is the onely paine will force their stout hearts to cry; I cannot heare of any disease of the stone amongst them (the corne of the Countrey, with which they are fed from the wombe, being an admirable cleanser and opener:) but the paine of their womens childbirth (of which I shall speake afterward in the Chapter of *Marriage*) never forces their women so to cry, as I have heard some of their men in this paine.

In this paine they use a certaine root dried, not much unlike our *Ginger*.

Sítchipuck.	*The necke.*
Quttuck.	*The throat.*
Timequássin.	*To cut off* or *behead.*

which they are most skilfull to doe in fight: for, when ever they wound, and their arrow sticks in the body of their enemie they (if they be valourous, and possibly may) they follow their arrow, and falling upon the person wounded and tearing his head a little aside by his Locke, they in the twinckling of an eye

fetch

fetch off his head though but with a sorry knife.

I know the man yet living, who in time of warre, pretended to fall from his owne campe to the enemie, proffered his service in the front with them against his own Armie from whence he had revolted. Hee propounded such plausible advantages, that he drew them out to battell, himselfe keeping in the front; but on a sudden, shot their chiefe Leader and Captaine, and being shot, in a trice fetcht off his head, and returned immediatly to his own againe, from whom in pretence (though with this trecherous intention) hee had revolted: his act was false and trecherous, yet herein appeares policie, stoutnesse and activitie, &c.

Mapànnog.	*The breast.*
Wuppíttene énash.	*Arme, Armes.*
Wuttàh.	*The heart.*
Wunnêtu nittà.	*My heart is good.*

Obs. This speech they use when ever they professe their honestie; they naturally confessing that all goodnesse is first in the heart.

Mishquínash.	*The vaines.*
Mishquè, néepuck.	*The blood.*
Uppusquàn.	*The backe.*
Nuppusquànnick.	*My back,* or *at my back.*

Wunníche-

Wunnícheke.	*Hand.*
Wunnickégannash.	*Hands.*
Mokássuck.	*Nayles.*

Ob. They are much delighted after battell to hang up the hands and heads of their enemies: (Riches, long Life, and the Lives of enemies being objects of great delight to all men naturall; but *Salomon* begg'd Wisedome before these.)

Wunnáks.	*The bellie.*
Apòme, Apòmash.	*The thigh, the thighs.*
Mohcônt, tash.	*A legge, legs.*
Wussète, tash.	*A foot, feet.*
Wunnichéganash.	*The toes.*
Tou wuttínsin.	*What manner of man?*
Tou núckquaque.	*Of what bignesse?*
Wompésu Mowêsu, & Suckêsu.	*White, Blacke,* or *swarfish.*

Obs. Hence they call a *Blackamore* (themselves are tawnie, by the Sunne and their annoyntings, yet they are borne white:)

Suckáutacone,	*A cole-blacke man.*

For, *Sucki* is black, and *Waûtacone*, one that weares clothes, whence *English*, *Dutch*, *French*, *Scotch*, they call *Wautaconâuog*, or *Coatmen*.

Cummínakese.	*You are strong.*
Minikêsu.	*Strong.*

Miniocquêsu

Minioquêsu.	*Weake.*
Cummíniocquese.	*Weake you are.*
Qunnaúqussu.	*A tall man.*
Qunnauqussítchick.	*Tall men.*
Tiaquónqussu.	*Low and short.*
Tiaquonqussíchick.	*Men of lowe stature.*
Wunnêtu-wock.	*Proper and personall.*

The generall Observation from the parts of the bodie.

Nature knowes no difference between *Europe* and *Americans* in blood, birth, bodies, &c. God having of one blood made all mankind, *Acts* 17. and all by nature being children of wrath, *Ephes.* 2.

More particularly:

Bòast not proud Euglish, *of thy birth & blood,*
   Thy brother Indian *is by birth as Good.*
Of one blood God made Him, and Thee & All,
   As wise, as faire, as strong, as personall.
By nature wrath's his portiõ, thine no more (store
   Till Grace his soule and thine *in Christ re-*
Make sure thy second birth, else thou shalt see,
   Heaven ope to Indians *wild, but shut to thee.*

Portion
(Restore)

E 3   C H A P.

Chap. VIII.

Of *Discourse* and *Newes*.

Aunchemokau-hettíttea. | *Let us discourse*, or *tell newes*.
Tocketeaunchim? | *What newes?*
Aaunchemókaw. | *Tell me your newes.*
Cuttaunchemókous. | *I will tell you newes.*
Mautaunchemokou-êan. | *When I have done telling the newes.*
Cummautaunche-mókous. | *I have done my newes.*

Obs. Their desire of, and delight in newes, is great, as the *Athenians*, and all men, more or lesse; a stranger that can relate newes in their owne language, they will stile him *Manitióo*, a God.

Wutaunchéocouôog. | *I will tell it them.*
Awaun mesh aunche-mókau. | *Who brought this newes?*
Awaun mesh kuppít-touwaw. | *Of whom did you heare it?*
Uppanáunchim. | *Your newes is true.*
Cowawwunnâun-chim. | *He tells false newes.*

Nummau-

Nummautanùme.	*I have spoken enough.*
Nsouwussánneme	*I am weary with speaking*

Obs. Their manner is upon any tidings to sit round double or treble or more, as their numbers be; I have seene neer a thousand in a round, where *English* could not well neere halfe so many have sitten: Every man hath his pipe of their *Tobacco,* and a deepe silence they make, and attention give to him that speaketh; and many of them will deliver themselves either in a relation of news, or in a consultation with very emphaticall speech and great action, commonly an houre, and sometimes two houres together.

Npenowauntawâu-men.	*I cannot speak your language.*
Matta nippánnawem	*I lie not.*
Cuppánnowem.	*You lie.*
Mattanickogga-choùsk	
Matntianta-cómpaw.	*I am no lying fellow.*
Matntiantá-sampáwwa.	
Achienonâumwem.	*I speake very true.*
Kukkita.	*Hearken to me.*
Kukkakittoùs.	*I heare you.*

Obs. They are impatient (as all men and God himselfe is) when their speech is not attended and listened to.

Cuppíttous.	*I understand you.*
Cowâutous.	
Machagenowâutam.	*I understand not.*
Matnowawtawaté-mina.	*Wee undestand not each other.*
Wunnâumwash.	*Speake the truth.*
Coanâumwem.	*You speake true.*

Obs. This word and and the next, are words of great flattery which they use each to other, but constantly to their Princes at their speeches, for which, if they be eloquent, they esteeme them Gods, as *Herod* among the *Iewes*.

Wunnâumwaw ewò.	*He speaks true.*
Cuppannawâutous.	*I doe not believe you.*
Cuppannawâuti?	*Doe you not believe?*
Nippannawâutunck ewò.	*He doth not believe me.*
Michéme nippanna-wâutam.	*I shall never believe it.*

Obs. As one answered me when I had discoursed about many points of God, of the creation, of the soule, of the danger of it, and the saving of it, he assented; but when I spake of the rising againe of the body, he cryed out, I shall never believe this.

Pannówa

Pannóuwa awàun, awaun keesitteóuwin.	*Some body hath made this lie.*
Tattâ Pìtch	*I cannot tell, it may so come to passe.*
Nni, eíu	*It is true.*
Mat enâno, *or,* mat eâno.	*It is not true.*
Kekuttokâunta.	*Let us speake together.*
Kuttókash.	*Speake.*
Tawhitch mat cuttôan?	*Why speake you not?*
Téaqua ntúnnawem, *or,* ntéawem?	*What should I speake?*
Wetapímmin.	*To sit downe.*
Wetapwâuwwas.	*Sit and talke with us.*
Taúpowaw.	*A wise speaker.*
Enapwáuwwaw, Eississûmo.	*He speaks* Indian.
Matta nowawwâuon, matta nowáhea.	*I know nothing of it.*
Pitchnowáuwon, Wunnaumwâuonck.	*I shall know the truth.*
Wunnaumwáyean.	*If he say true.*

Obs. Canounicus, the old high *Sachim* of the *Nariganset Bay* (a wise and peaceable Prince) once in a solemne Oration to my self, in a solemne assembly, using this word, said, I have

never

never suffered any wrong to be offered to the
English since they landed; nor never will: he
often repeated this word, *Wunnaumwáyean*,
Englishman; if the *Englishman* speake true, if
hee meane truly, then shall I goe to my grave
in peace, and hope that the *English* and my posteritie shall live in love and peace together. I
replied, that he had no cause (as I hoped) to
question *Englishmans, Wunnaumwaúonck*, that
is, faithfulnesse, he having had long experience
of their friendlinesse and trustinesse. He tooke
a sticke and broke it into ten pieces, and related
ten instances (laying downe a sticke to every
instance) which gave him cause thus to feare
and say; I satisfied him in some presently, and
presented the rest to the Governours of the
English, who, I hope, will be far from giving
just cause to have *Barbarians* to question their
Wunnaumwâuonck, or faithfulnesse.

Tocketunnántum, Tocketunáname, Tocketeántam?	*What doe you thinke?*
Ntunnántum, Nteántum.	*I thinke.*
Nánick nteeâtum.	*I thinke so to.*
Nteatámmowonck.	*That is my thought,* or *opinion*
Matntunnantámmen Matnteeantámmen.	*I thinke not so.* Nowecón-

Nowecóntam,	*I am glad.*
Noweeteántam.	
Coanáumatous.	*I believe you.*

Obs. This word they use just as the *Greeke* tongue doth that verbe, πιsέυειν: for believing or obeying as it is often used in the new *Testament,* and they say *Coannáumatous,* I will obey you.

Yo aphéttit.	*When they are here.*
Yo peyáhettit.	*When they are com.*

This Ablative case absolute they much use, and comprise much in little;

Awaunagrss, suck	*English-man, men.*

This they call us, as much as to say, These strangers.

Waútacone-nûaog.	*Englishman, men.*

That is, Coat-men, *or* clothed.

Cháuquaqock.	*English-men,* properly sword-men.
Wautacónisk.	*An English woman.*
Wautaconémese.	*An English youth.*
Wáske peyáeyan.	*When you came first.*
Wáske peyáhetit,	*When English-men*
Wautaconâuog.	*came first.*
Táwhitch peyáhettit	*Why come they hither?*

Obs. This question they oft put to me: Why come the *Englishmen* hither? and measuring others by themselves; they say, It is because

you

you want *firing:* for they, having burnt up
the *wood* in one place, (wanting draughts to
bring *wood* to them) they are faine to follow
the *wood;* and so to remove to a fresh new
place for the *woods* sake.

Matta mihtuckqun- núnno?	*Have you no trees?*
Mishàunetash, Màunetash.	*Great store.*
Maunâuog, Wussaumemaunâuog Noonapúock.	*They are too full of people.* *They have not roome one by another.*
Aumáumuwaw Páuasha.	*A messenger comes.*
Wawwhawtowâuog.	*They hollow.*
Wauwhaûtowaw ánawat.	*'Tis an Alarme.*

Obs. If it be in time of *warre*, he that is a
Messenger runs swiftly, and at every towne the
Messenger comes, a fresh *Messenger* is sent:
he that is the last, comming within a mile or
two of the Court, or chiefe house, he *hollowes*
often and they that heare answer him untill
by mutuall *hollowing* and answering hee is
brought to the place of *audience*, whereby this
meanes is gathered a great confluence of people to entertaine the *newes*.

Wussúck-

| Wussuckwhèke, | *A letter which they so* |
| Wussúckwhonck. | *call from* Wussuck- |

whómmin, to paint; for, having no letters, their painting comes the neerest.

| Wussúckquash. | *Write a Letter.* |
| Wússuckwheke, yímmi. | *Make me a Letter.* |

Obs. That they have often desired of me upon many occasions; for their good and peace, and the *English* also, as it hath pleased God to vouchsafe opportunitie.

Quenowâuog.	*They complaine.*
Tawhitch quená-wáyean?	*Why complaine you?*
Muccò.	*It is true you say.*
Tuckawntéawem?	*What should I say to it?*

The generall *Observation* from their *Discourse* and *Newes*

The whole race of *mankind* is generally infected with an *itching desire* of hearing *Newes*.

more particular:

1 Mans *restlesse soule hath restlesse eyes and eares, Wanders in* change *of sorrows, cares and feares.*   *Faine*

Faine would it (Bee-like) *suck by the ears,*
    by the eye
Something that might his hunger satisfie:
The Gospel, *or* Glad tidings *onely can,*
Make glad the English, *and the* Indian.

Chap. IX.
Of *the time of the day.*

Obs. THey are punctuall in measuring their *Day* by the *Sunne*, and their *Night* by the *Moon* and the *Starres*, and their lying much abroad in the ayre; and so living in the open fields, occasioneth even the youngest amongst them to be very observant of those *Heavenly* Lights.

Mautáubon, Chich-áuquat wompan.	*It is day.*
Aumpatâuban.	*It is broad day.*
Tou wuttúttan?	*How high is the Sunne?* that is, *What is't a clocke?*
Páspisha.	*It is Sunne-rise.*
Nummáttaquaw.	*Fore-noone.*
Yáhen Páushaquaw.	*Allmost noone.*
Páweshaquaw.	*Noone.*
Quttúkquaquaw Panicómpaw.	*After dinner.*

Naw-

Nawwâuwquaw.	*After-noone.*
Yo wuttúttan.	*The Sunne thus high.*
Yáhen waiyàuw.	*Allmost Sun-set.*
Wayaàwi.	*The Sun is set.*
Wunnáuquit:	*Evening.*
Póppakunnetch, au-cháugotch.	*Darke night.*
Túppaco, & Otematíppocat.	*Toward night.*
Nanashowatíppocat.	*Midnight.*
Chouóeatch.	*About Cockcrowing.*
Kitompanisha.	*Breake of day.*
Yò taunt nippéean.	*The Sun thus high, I will come.*

Obs. They are punctuall in their promises of keeping time; and sometimes have charged mee with a lye for not punctually keeping time, though hindred.

Yo tàunt cuppee-yâumen.	*Come by the Sunne thus high.*
Anamakéesuck.	*This day.*
Saûop.	*To morrow.*
Wussâume tátsha.	*It is too late.*
Tiaquockaskéesakat.	*A short day.*
Quawquonikéesakat.	*A long day.*
Quawquonikeesaqút-cheas.	*Long dayes.*

Nquit-

Nquittakeesiquóckat, Nquittakeespúmmi- shen.	*One dayes walke.*
Paukúnnum.	*Darke.*
Wequâi.	*Light.*
Wequáshim.	*Moon-light.*

The generall observation from their time
of the day.

The *Sunne* and *Moone,* in the observation
of all the *sonnes* of *men,* even the wildest are
the great *Directors* of the *day* and *night;* as it
pleased *God* to appoint in the first *Creation.*

More particular.
1 *The* Indians *find the* Sun *so sweet,*
   He is a God *they say;*
Giving them Light, *and* Heat, *and* Fruit,
   And Guidance *all the day.*
2 *They have no helpe of* Clock *or* Watch,
   And Sunne *they* overprize.
Having those artificiall helps, the Sun,
   We unthankfully despise.   (*more bright*
God *is a* Sunne *and* Shield, *a thousand times*
   Indians, *or* English, *thongh they see.*
   Yet how few prise his Light?

C H A P .

Chap. X.

Of *the season of the Yeere.*

NQuittaqúnnegat.	*One day.*
Neesqúnnagat.	2 *dayes.*
Shuckqunóckat.	3 *dayes.*
Yowunnóckat, &c.	4 *dayes.*
Piuckaqúnnagat.	10 *dayes.*
Piuckaqunnagat nab-naquìt.	11 *dayes.*
Piuckaqúnnagat nab neeze, *&c.*	12 *dayes*
Neesneechektashuck qunnóckat.	20 *dayes*
Neesneechektashuck qunnockat-nabna-quìt, &c.	21 *dayes.*
Séquan.	*The Spring.*
Aukeeteámitch.	
Néepun, *&*	*Spring,* or *Seed-time.*
Quaqúsquan.	*Summer.*
Taquònck.	*Fall of leafe and An-tumne.*
Papòne.	*Winter.*
Saséquacup.	*This Spring last.*

Yo neepúnnacup.	*This Summer last.*
Yò taquónticup.	*This Harvest last.*
Papapôcup.	*Winter last.*
Yaûnedg.	*The last yeere.*
Nippaûus.	*The Sunne.*
Munnánnock.	
Nanepaûshat.	*The Moone.*
Nqnitpawsuckenpaû-us.	1 *Moneth.*
Neespausuck npaûus.	2 *Moneths.*
Shwe pausuck npaû-us &c.	3 *Moneths.*
Neesneáhettit	2 *Moneths.*
Shwinneáhettit.	3 *Moneths.*
Yowinneáhettit, &c.	4 *Moneths.*

Obs. They have thirteen *Moneths* according to the severall *Moones*; and they give to each of them significant names: *as,*

Sequanakéeswush.	*Spring moneth.*
Neepunnakéeswush.	*Summer moneth.*
Taquontikéeswush.	*Harvest moneth.*
Paponakéeswush, &c.	*Winter moneth, &c.*
Nquittecautúmmo.	1 *Yeere.*
Tashecautúmmo?	*How many yeeres?*
Chashecautúmmo cuttáppemus?	*How many yeeres since you were borne?*
Neesecautúmmo.	2 *Yeere.*
Shwecautúmmo.	3 *Yeere.*

Yowecau-

Yowecautúmmo.	4 *Yeere.*
Piukquecautúmmo.	10 *Yeere.*
Piuckquecautúmmo, nabnaquìt, &c.	11 *Yeere, &c.*

Obs. If the yeere proove drie, they have great and solemne meetings from all parts at one high place, to supplicate their gods; and to beg raine, and they will continue in this worship ten days, a fortnight; yea, three weekes, untill raine come.

Tashínash papónash?	*How many winters?*
Ahauqushapapòne.	*A sharpe winter.*
Kéesqush keesuck-quâi.	*By day.*
Náukocks nokan-náwi.	*By night.*

Generall Observation *from their* Seasons
of the Yeere.

The *Sunne* and *Moone*, and *Starres* and *seasons* of the yeere doe preach a *God* to all the sonnes of men, that they which know no letters, doe yet read an *eternall Power* and *Godhead* in these:

More speciall.

The Sun *and* Moone *and* Stars *doe preach,*
The Dayes *and* Nights *found out:*

Spring

Spring, Summer, Fall, *and* Winter *eke*
Each Moneth *and* Yeere *about*.
2   *So that the* wildest *sonnes of men*
Without excuse shall say,
Gods righteous *sentence past on us*,
(*In dreadfull Judgement day.*)
If so, what doome is theirs that see,
Not onely Natures *light*;
But Sun *of* Righteousnesse, *yet chose*
To live in darkest Night?

Chap. XI.

Of Travell.

Máyi.	*Away.*
Mayúo?	*Is there a way?*
Mat mayanúnno.	*There is no way.*
Peemáyagat.	*A little way.*
Mishimmayagat.	*A great path.*
Machípscat.	*A stone path.*

Obs. It is admirable to see, what paths their naked hardned feet have made in the wildernesse in most stony and rockie places.

Nnatotemúckaun.	*I will aske the way.*
Kunnatótemous.	*I will inquire of you.*
Kunnatotemì?	*Doe you aske me?*

Tou

Tou nishin méyi?	*Where lies the way?*
Kokotemíinnea méyi	*Shew me the way.*
Yo áinshick méyi.	*There the way lies.*
Kukkakótemous.	*I will shew you.*
Yo cummittamáyon.	*There is the way you must goe.*
Yo chippachâusin.	*There the way divides.*
Maúchatea.	*A guide.*
Máuchase.	*Be my guide.*

Obs. The wildernesse being so vast, it is a mercy, that for a hire a man shall never want guides, who will carry provisions, and such as hire them over the Rivers and Brookes, and find out often times hunting-houses, or other lodgings at night.

Anòce wénawash.	*Hire him.*
Kuttánnoonsh.	*I will hire you.*
Kuttaúnckquitta-unch.	*I will pay you.*
Kummuchickónck-quatous.	*I will pay you well.*
Tocketaonckquittíin-nea.	*What wil you give me?*
Cummáuchanish.	*I will conduct you.*
Yò aûnta,	*Let us goe that way.*
Yò cuttâunan.	*Goe that way.*
Yo mtúnnock.	*The right hand.*
Yo nmúnnatch.	*The left hand.*

Cowéchaush.	*I will goe with you.*
Wétash.	*Goe along.*
Cowéchaw ewò.	*He will goe with you.*
Cowechauatímmin.	*I will goe with you.*
Wechauatíttea.	*Let us accompany.*
Taûbot wétáyean.	*I thanke you for your company.*

Obs. I have heard of many *English* lost, and have oft been lost my selfe, and my selfe and others have often been found, and succoured by the *Indians*.

Pitchcowáwwon.	*You will lose your way.*
Meshnowáwwon.	*I lost my way.*
Nummauchèmin, Ntanniteímmin.	*I will be going.*
Mammauchêtuck.	*Let us be going.*
ânakiteunck. Memauchêwi ánittui.	*He is gone.*
Memauchegushán- nick.	*They are gone.*
Anakugushánnick.	*They are gone.*
Tunnockkuttòme Tunnockkuttoyeâim Tunnockkuttínshem.	*Whither goe you?*
Nnegónshem.	*I will goe before.*
Cuppompáish.	*I will stay for you.*
Negónshesh.	*Goe before.*
Mittummayaûcup.	*The way you went be- fore.* Cummat-

Cummáttanish.	*I will follow you.*
Cuppahímmin.	*Stay for me.*
Tawhich quaunqua quêan.?	*Why doe you run so?*
Nowecóntum púmmishem.	*I have a mind to travell*
Konkenuphshâuta.	*Let us goe apace.*
Konkenúppe.	*Goe apace.*
Michéme nquaunquaquêmin.	*I have run alwayes.*
Yo ntoyamâushem.	*I goe this pace.*

Obs. They are generally quick on foot, brought up from the breasts to running: their legs being also from the wombe stretcht and bound up in a strange way on their Cradle backward, as also annointed; yet have they some that excell: so that I have knowne many of them run betweene fourscore or an hundred miles in a Summers day, and back within two dayes: they doe also practice running of *Races*; and commonly in the Summer, they delight to goe without shoes, although they have them hanging at their backs: they are so exquisitely skilled in all the body and bowels of the Countrey (by reason of their huntings) that I have often been guided twentie, thirtie, sometimes fortie miles through the woods, a streight course out of any path.

F 4 Yò

Yò wuchê.	*From hence.*
Tounúckquaque yo wuchê	*How far from hence?*
Yò anúckquaque.	*So farre.*
Yo anuckquaquêse.	*So little a way.*
Waunaquêse.	*A little way.*
Aukeewushaûog.	*They goe by land.*
Míshoon hómwock.	*They goe* or *come by water.*
Naynayoûmewot.	*A Horse.*
Wunnìa, naynayoû-mewot.	*He rides on Horse-back.*

Obs. Having no Horses, they covet them above other Cattell, rather preferring ease in riding, then their profit and belly, by milk and butter from Cowes and Goats and they are loth to come to the *English* price for any.

Aspumméwi	*He is not gone by.*
As pumméwock	*They are not gone by.*
Awanick payánchick	*Who come there?*
Awanick negonsha-chick?	*Who are these before us?*
Yo cuppummesicóm min.	*Crosse over into the way there.*
Cuppì-machàug.	*Thick wood : a Swamp.*

Obs. These thick Woods and Swamps (like the Boggs to the *Irish*) are the Refuges for Women and children in Warre, whil'st the
men

men fight. As the Country is wondrous full of Brookes and Rivers, so doth it also abound with fresh ponds, some of many miles compasse.

Níps-nipsash	*Pond : Ponds.*
Wèta: wétedg	*The Woods : on fire.*
Wussaumpatámmin	*To view or looke about.*
Wussaum patámo- onck.	*A Prospect.*
Wuttocékémin	*To wade.*
Tocekétuck	*Let us wade.*
Tou wuttáuqusfin?	*How deepe?*
Yò ntaúqusfin	*Thus deep.*
Kunníish.	*I will carry you.*
Kuckqússuckqun	*You are heavy.*
Kunnâukon	*You are light.*
Pasúckquish	*Rise.*
Anakish : maúchish:	*Goe.*
Quaquìsh	*Runne.*
Nokus káuatees	*Meet him.*
Nockuskauatítea	*Let us meet.*
Necnmcshnóckuskaw.	*I did meet.*

Obs. They are joyfull in meeting of any in travell, and will strike fire either with stones or sticks, to take Tobacco, and discourse a little together.

Mesh

Mesh Kunnockqus kauatímmin?	*Did you meet?* *&c.*
Yo Kuttauntapím- min.	*Let us rest here.*
Kussackquêtuck.	*Let us sit downe.*
Yo appíttuck Nissówanis	*Let us sit here.*
Nissowànishkaû men.	*I am weary.*
Nickqússaqus	*I am lame.*
Ntouagonnausinnúm min	*We are distrest undone, or in misery.*

Obs. They use this word properly in wandring toward Winter night, in which case I have been many a night with them, and many times also alone yet alwayes mercifully preserved.

Teâno wonck nippée am	*I will be here by and by againe.*
Mat Kunníckansh	*I will not leave you.*
Aquie Kunnickat- shash.	*Doe not leave me.*
Tavvhítch nickat shiêan?	*Why doe you forsake me?*
Wuttánho	*A staffe.*
Yò íish Wuttánho	*Use this staffe.*

Obs.

Obs. Sometimes a man shall meet a lame man or an old man with a Staffe: but generally a Staffe is a rare sight in the hand of the eldest, their Constitution is so strong. I have upon occasion travelled many a score, yea many a hundreth mile amongst them, without need of stick or staffe, for any appearance of danger amongst them: yet it is a rule amongst them, that it is not good for a man to travell without a Weapon nor alone.

Taquáttin	*Frost.*
Auke taquátsha	*The ground is frozen.*
Séip taquáttin.	*The River is frozen.*
Nowánnesin	*I have forgotten.*
nippitt akúnna mun.	*I must goe back.*

Obs. I once travalled with neere 200 who had word of neere 700. Enemies in the way, yet generally they all resolved that it was a shame to feare and goe back.

Nippanishkokómmin Npussàgo. kommìn	*I have let fall something.*
Mattaâsu	*A little way.*
Naûwot.	*A great way.*
Náwwatick	*Farre of at Sea.*
Ntaquatchuwaûmen	*I goe up hill.*
	Taguatchòwash

Taguatchòwash	*Goe up hill.*
Wàumsu	*Downe hill.*
Mauúnshesh	*Goe slowly or gently.*
Mauanisháuta	*Let us goe gently.*
Tawhìtch cheche qunnuwáyean?	*Why doe you rob me?*
Aquie chechequnnúwash.	*Doe not rob me.*
Chechequnnuwáchick.	*Robbers.*
Chechequnníttin	*There is a Robbery committed.*
Kemineantúock	*They murder each other.*

Obs. If any Robbery fall out in Travell, between Person of diverse States, the offended State sends for Justice, If no Justice bee granted and recompence made, they grant out a kind of Letter of Mart to take satisfaction themselues, yet they are carefull not to exceed in taking from others, beyond the Proportion of their owne losse.

Wúskont àwaùn nkemineíucqun.	*I feare some will murther mee.*

Obs. I could never heare that Murthers or Robberies are comparably so frequent, as in parts of *Europe* amongst the English, French, &c.

Cutchachewussím.

Cutchachewussím min.	*You are almost there.*
Kiskecuppeeyāumen.	*You are a little short.*
Cuppeeyáumen	*Now you are there.*
Muckquétu	*Swift.*
Cummúmmuckquete.	*You are swift.*
Cussásaqus	*You are slow.*
Sassaqushâuog	*They are slow.*
Cuttinneapúmmishem	*Will you passe by?*
Wuttineapummushâuta.	*Let us passe by.*
Keeatshaûta.	*I come for no busines.*
Ntinneapreyaûmen	
Acoûwe	*In vaine or to no purpose.*
Ntackówvvepeyaùn.	*I have lost my labour.*
Cummautûssakou.	*You have mist him.*
Kihtummâyi-wussáuhumwi.	*He went just now forth.*
Pittúckish.	*Goe back.*
Pittuckétuck.	*Let us goe back.*
Pónewhush.	*Lay downe your burthen.*

Generall

Generall Observations of their Travell.

A s the same Sun shines on the Wildernesse
that doth on a Garden ! so the same
faithfull and all sufficient God, can comfort-
feede and safely guide even through a deso-
late howling Wildernesse.

More particular.

God makes a Path, provides a Guide,
   And feeds in Wildernesse !
1 *His glorious Name while breath remaines,*
   O that I may confesse.

Lost many a time, I have had no Guide,
2 *No House, but hollow Tree !*
 In stormy VVinter night no Fire,
   No Food, no Company:

In him I have found a House, a Bed,
3 *A Table, Company:*
 No Cup so bitter, but's made sweet,
   VVhen Go'd shall Sweetning be.

CHAP. III.

Chap. XII.

Concerning the Heavens and Heavenly Lights,

Kéesuck.	*The Heavens.*
Keesucquíu.	*Heavenward.*
Aúke, Aukeeaseíu.	*Downwards.*
Nippâwus.	*The Sun.*
Keesuckquànd.	*A name of the Sun.*

(Obs.) By which they acknowledge the Sun, and adore for a God or divine power.

Munnánnock.	*A name of the Sun.*
Nanepaùshat, & Munnánnock. }	*The Moone.*
Wequáshim.	*A light Moone.*
Pashpíshea.	*The Moone is up.*
Yo wuttúttan.	*So high.*

Obs. And so they use the same rule, and words for the course of the Moone in the *Night*, as they use for the course of the Sun by *Day*, which wee mentioned in the Chapter of the Houre, or time of the Day concerning the Sunnes rising , course, or Sunne setting.

Yò

Yò Ockquitteunk.	*A new Moone.*
Paushésui.	*Halfe Moone.*
Yo wompanámmit.	

Obs. The Moone so old, which they mea-
sure by the setting of it, especially when it
shines till *Wómpan,* or day.

Anóckqus: anócksuck. | *A Starre Starres.*

Obs. By occasion of their frequent lying in
the Fields and Woods, they much observe
the Starres, and their very children can give
Names to many of them, and observe their
Motions, and they have the same words for
their rising-courses and setting, as for the
Sun or Moone, as before.

Mosk or *Paukúnawaw* the great Beare, or
Charles Waine, which words *Mosk,* or *Pau-
kúnnawwáw* signifies a Beare, which is so
much the more observable, because, in most
Languages that signe or Constellation is called
the Beare.

Shwishcuttowwáuog	*The Golden Metewand.*
Mishánnock.	*The morning Starre.*
Chippápuock.	*The Brood-hen, &c.*

*Generall Observations of the Heauenly
Bodies.*

The wildest sons of Men heare the preaching

ing of the Heavens, the Sun, Moone, and
Starres, yet not seeking after God the Maker
are justly condemned, though they never
have nor despise other preaching, as the ci-
viliz'd World hath done.

More particular.

When Sun doth rise the Starres doe set,
　Yet there's no need of Light,
God shines a Sunne *most glorious,*
　When Creatures all are Night.

The very Indian *Boyes can give,*
　To many Starres *their name,*
And know their Course and therein doe,
　2. *Excell the* English *tame.*

　　3　English *and* Indians *none enquire,*
　　　Whose hand these Candles hold:
Job. 35. *Who gives these* Stars *their Names*
　　　More bright ten thousand fold. (himself

G　Chap. XIII.

Chap. XIII.

Of the Weather.

TOcke tussinnám-min kéesuck?	*What thinke you of the Weather?*
Wekineaûquat.	*Faire Weather.*
Wekinnàuquocks.	*When it is faire weather.*
Tahkì, *or* tátakki.	*Cold weather.*
Tahkeès.	*Cold,*

Obs. It may bee wondred why since *New-England* is about 12. degrees neerer to the Sun, yet some part of Winter it is there ordinarily more cold then here in *Englands*: the reason is plaine: All Ilands are warmer then maine Lands and Continents, *England* being an Iland, *Englands* winds are Sea winds, which are commonly more thick and vapoury, and warmer winds: The *Nor West* wind (which occcasioneth *New-England* cold) comes over the cold frozen Land, and over many millions of Loads of Snow: and yet the pure wholsomnesse of the Aire is wonderfull, and the warmth of the Sunne, such in the sharpest weather, that I have often seen the Natives Children runne about starke naked in

the

the coldest dayes, and the *Indians* Men and
Women lye by a Fire, in the Woods in the
coldest nights, and I have been often out my
selfe such nights without fire, mercifully, and
wonderfully preserved.

Taúkocks.	*Cold weather.*
Káusitteks.	*Hot weather.*
Kussúttah.	*It is hot.*
Núckqusquatch nnóonakom.	*I am a cold.*
Nickqussittâunum.	*I Sweat.*
Mattâuqus.	*A cloud.*
Máttaquat.	*It is over-cast.*
Cúppaquat.	
Sókenun. ánaquat.	*Raine.*
Anamakéesuck sókenun.	*It will raine to-day.*
Sókenitch.	*When it raines.*
Sóchepo, *or* Cône.	*Snow.*
Animanâukock-Sóchepo.	*It will snow to night.*
Sóchepwutch.	*When it snowes.*
Mishúnnan.	*A great raine.*
Pâuqui, pâuquaquat.	*It holds up.*
Nnáppi.	*Drie.*
Nnáppaqnat.	*Drie weather.*
Tópu.	*A frost.*

Missittópu.

Missittópu.	*A great Frost.*
Capát.	*Ice.*
Néechipog.	*The Deaw.*
Míchokat.	*A Thaw.*
Míchokateh.	*When it thawes.*
Missuppâugatch.	*When the rivers are open.*
Cutshâusha.	*The Lightning.*
Neimpâuog.	*Thunder.*
Neimpâuog pesk hómwock.	*Thunderbolts are shot.*

Obs. From this the Natives conceiving a consimilitude between our Guns and Thunder, they call a Gunne *Péskunck,* and to discharge *Peskhómmin* that is to thunder.

 Observation generall of the VVeather.

That Judgement which the Lord Jesus pronounced against the Weather-wise (but ignorant of the God of the weather) will fall most justly upon those *Natives,* and all men who are wise in Naturall things, but willingly blind in spirituall.

 English *and* Indians *spie a Storme,*
  and seeke a hiding place:
 O hearts of stone that thinke and dreame,
  Th'everlasting stormes t'out-face.
 Proud filthy Sodome *saw the Sunne,*
  Shine or'e her head most bright.

      The

The very day that turn'd she was
To stincking heaps, 'fore night.
How many millions now alive,
VVithin few yeeres shall rot?
O blest that Soule, *whose portion is,*
That Rocke *that changeth not.*

Chap. XIV.

Of *the Winds.*

VVAûpi.	*The Wind.*
Wâupanash.	*The Winds.*
Tashínash wáupanash	*How many winds are there?*

Obs. Some of them account of seven, some eight, or nine; and in truth, they doe upon the matter reckon and observe not onely the foure but the eight Cardinall winds, although they come not to the accurate division of the 32. upon the 32. points of the compasse, as we doe.

Nanúmmatin, & Sunnâdin.	*The North wind.*
Chepewéssin.	*The North east.*
Sáchimoachepewéssin.	*Strong North east wind.*

G 3 Nopâtin

Nopâtin.	*The East wind.*
Nanóckquittin	*The South east wind.*
Touwúttin	*South wind.*
Papônetin	*West wind.*
Chékesu	*The Northwest.*
Chékesitch	*When the wind blowes Northwest.*
Tocketunnántum?	*What thinke you?*
Tou pìtch wuttìn?	*Where wil the wind be?*
Nqénouhìck wuttìn	*I stay for a wind.*
Yo pìtch wuttìn Sâuop	*Here the wind will be to morrow.*
Pìtch Sowwánishen.	*It will be Southwest.*

Obs. This is the pleasingest, warmest wind in the Climate, most desired of the *Indians,* making faire weather ordinarily; and therefore they have a *Tradition,* that to the Southwest, which they call *Sowwaniu,* the gods chiefly dwell; and hither the soules of all their Great and Good men and women goe.

This Southwest wind is called by the *New-English,* the Sea turne, which comes from the Sunne in the morning, about nine or ten of the clock Southeast, and about South, and then strongest Southwest in the after-noone, and towards night, when it dies away.

It is rightly called the Sea turne, because the wind commonly all the Summer, comes

off

off from the North and Northwest in the night, and then turnes againe about from the South in the day: as *Salomon* speaks of the vanitie of the Winds in their changes, *Eccles.* 1-6.

Mishâupan	*A great wind.*
Mishitáshin	*A storme.*
Wunnágehan, *or,*	*Faire wind.*
Wunnêgin waúpi.	
Wunnêgitch wuttìn	*When the wind is faire.*
Mattágehan	*A crosse wind.*
Wunnágehatch	*When the wind comes fair*
Mattágehatch	*When the wind is crosse.*
Cowunnagehúcka-men.	*You have a faire wind.*
Cummattagehúcka-men.	*The wind is against you.*
Nummattagehúcka-men.	*The wind is against mee.*

Generall Observations *of the* Winds.

God is wonderfully glorious in bringing the *Winds* out of his Treasure, and riding upon the wings of those *Winds* in the eyes of all the sonnes of men in all Coasts of the world.

More particular:

1 English *and* Indian *both observe,*
  The various blasts of wind:

G 4   *And*

And both I have heard in dreadfull stormes
  Cry out aloud, I have sinn'd.

But when the stormes are turn'd to calmes,
  And seas grow smooth and still:
Both turne (like Swine) *to wallow in,*
  The filth of former will.

'Tis not a storme on sea, or shore,
  'Tis not the VVord *that can;*
But 'tis the Spirit *or* Breath *of* God
  That must renew the man.

CHAP. XV.

Of *Fowle*.

N Pesháwog Pussekesèsuck.	*Fowle.*
Ntauchâumen.	*I goe afowling* or *hunting.*
Auchaûi.	*Hee is gone to hunt* or *fowle.*
Pepemôi.	*He is gone to fowle.*
Wómpissacuk.	*An Eagle.*
Wompsacuck quâuog.	*Eagle.*

Néhom,

Néyhom, mâuog.	*Turkies.*
Paupock, sûog.	*Partridges.*
Aunckuck, quâuog.	*Heath-cocks.*
Chógan, ēuck.	*Black-bird, Black-birds.*

Obs. Of this sort there be millions, which are great devourers of the *Indian* corne as soon as it appears out of the ground; Unto this sort of Birds, especially, may the mysticall Fowles, the Divells be well resembled (and so it pleaseth the Lord Jesus himselfe to observe, *Matth.* 13. which mysticall Fowle follow the sowing of the Word, and picke it up from loose and carelesse hearers, as these Black-birds follow the materiall feed.

Against the Birds the *Indians* are very carefull, both to set their corne deep enough that it may have a strong root, not so apt to be pluckt up, (yet not too deep, lest they bury it, and it never come up:) as also they put up little watch-houses in the middle of their fields, in which they, or their biggest children lodge, and earely in the morning prevent the Birds: &c.

Kokókehom,	*An Owle.*
Ohómous.	
Kaukont tuock.	*Crow, Crowes.*

Obs. These Birds, although they doe the corne also some hurt, yet scarce will one *Na-*
tive

tive amongst an hundred wil kil them because they have a tradition, that the Crow brought them at first an *Indian* Graine of Corne in one Eare, and an *Indian* or *French* Beane in another, from the Great God *Kautántouwits* field in the Southwest from whence they hold came all their Corne and Beanes.

Hònck,-hónckock, Wómpatuck-quâuog.	*Goose, Geese.*
Wéquash-shâuog.	*Swans, Swans.*
Munnùcks-munnùck suck.	*Brants,* or *Brantgeese.*
Quequēcum-mâuog.	*Ducks.*

Obs. The *Indians* having abundance of these sorts of Foule upon their waters, take great pains to kill any of them with their Bow and Arrowes; and are marvellous desirous of our *English* Guns, powder and shot (though they are wisely and generally denied by the *English*) yet with those which they get from the *French*, and some others (*Dutch* and *English*) they kill abundance of Fowle, being naturally excellent marks-men; and also more hardned to endure the weather, and wading, lying, and creeping on the ground, &c.

I once saw an exercise of training of the *English*, when all the *English* had mist the mark

set

set up to shoot at, an *Indian* with his owne
Peece (desiring leave to shoot) onely hit it.

| Kítsuog. | *Cormorants.* |

Obs. These they take in the night time,
where they are asleepe on rocks, off at Sea, and
bring in at break of day great store of them:

| Yo aquéchmock. | *There they swim.* |
| Nipponamouôog | *I lay nets for them.* |

Ob. This they doe on shore, and catch many
fowle upon the plaines, and feeding under
Okes upon *Akrons,* as Geese, Turkies, Cranes,
and others, &c.

Ptowễi.	*It is fled.*
Ptowewunshánnick.	*They are fled:*
Wunnùp,-pash	*Wing, Wings:*
Wunnúppaníck ánawhone	*Wing-shot:*
Wuhóckgock ânwhone	*Body-shot:*
Wuskówhàn	*A Pigeon:*
Wuskowhãnannûaog	*Pigeons:*
Wuskowhannanaûkit	*Pigeon Countrie:*

Obs. In that place these Fowle breed abun-
dantly, and by reason of their delicate Food
(especially in Strawberrie time when they
pick up whole large Fields of the old grounds
of the *Natives,* they are a delicate fowle, and
because of their abundance, and the facility
of

of killing of them, they are and may be plentifully fed on.

Sachim: a little Bird about the bignesse of
a swallow, or lesse, to which the *Indians* give
that name, because of its *Sachim* or Princelike
courage and Command over greater Birds,
that a man shall often see this small Bird pursue and vanquish and put to flight the Crow,
and other Birds farre bigger then it selfe.

Sowwánakitauwaw—*They go to the Southward.*

That is the saying of the *Natives,* when the
Geese and other Fowle at the approach of
Winter betake themselves, in admirable Order and discerning their Course even all the
night long.

Chepewâukitaúog   —*They fly Northward.*

That is when they returne in the Spring.
There are abundance of singing Birds whose
names I have little as yet inquired after, &c.

The *Indians* of *Martins* vineyard, at my late
being amongst them, report generally, and
confidently of some Ilands, which lie off
from them to Sea, from whence every morning early, certaine Fowles come and light a-
mongst them, and returne at Night to lodging, which Iland or Ilands are not yet discovered, though probably, by other Reasons
they give, there is Land, &c.

Taûnek-

Taûnek-kaûog. | *Crane, Cranes.*
Wushówunan. | *The Hawke.*

Whch the *Indians* keep tame about their houses to keepe the little Birds from their Corne.

The generall Observation of Fowle.

How sweetly doe all the severall sorts of Heaven Birds, in all Coasts of the World, preach unto Men the prayse of their Makers Wisedome , Power , and Goodnesse , who feedes them and their young ones Summer and Winter with their severall suitable sorts of Foode: although they neither sow nor reape, nor gather into Barnes?

More particularly:

If Birds that neither sow nor reape.
  Nor store up any food,
Constantly find to them and theirs
  A maker kind and Good!

If man provide eke for his Birds,
  In Yard, in Coops, in Cage.
And each Bird spends in songs and Tunes,
  His little time and Age!
What care will Man, what care will God,
                              For's

For's wife and Children take?
Millions of Birds and Worlds will God.
Sooner then His forsake.

Chap. XVI.

Of *the Earth, and the Fruits thereof, &c.*

Aûke, & Sanaukamúck.	Earth or Land.
Níttauke Nissawnâwkamuck.	My Land.
Wuskáukamuck.	New ground.
Aquegunnítteash.	Fields worne out.
Mihtúck-quash.	Trees.
Pauchautaqun-nêsash.	Branch, Branches.
Wunnèpog-guash.	Leafe, leaves.
Wattáp.	A root of Tree,
Séip.	A River.
Toyùsk.	A bridge.
Sepoêse.	A little River.
Sepoêmese.	A little Rivulet.
Takêkum.	A Spring.
Takekummûo?	Is there a Spring.

Sepûo?

| Sepûo? | *Is there a River?* |
| Toyusquanûo. | *Is there a Bridge.* |

Obs. The *Natives* are very exact and punctuall in the bounds of their Lands, belonging
to this or that Prince or People, (even to a
River, Brooke) &c. And I have knowne
them make bargaine and sale amongst themselves for a small piece , or quantity of
Ground: notwithstanding a sinfull opinion
amongst mauy that Christians have right to
Heathens Lands: but of the delusion of that
phrase, I have spoke in a discourse concerning the *Indians* Conversion.

Paugáutemisk.	*An Oake.*
Wómpimish.	*A Chesnut Tree.*
Wómpimineash.	*Chesnutts.*

Obs. The *Indians* have an Art of drying
their Chesnuts, and so to preserve them in
their barnes for a daintie all the yeare.

| Anáuchemineash. | *Akornes.* |

These Akornes also they drie, and in case
of want of Corne, by much boyling they
make a good dish of them: yea sometimes in
plentie of Corne doe they eate these Acornes
for a Novelty.

| Wússoquat. | *A Wallnut Tree.* |
| Wusswaquatómineug. | *Wallnut.* |

Of these Wallnuts they make an excellent
                                        Oyle

Oyle good for many uses, but especially for their annoynting of their heads. And of the chips of the Walnut-Tree (the barke taken off) some *English* in the Countrey make excellent Beere both for Tast, strength, colour, and in offensive opening operation:

Sasaunckapâmuck.	*The* Sassafrasse *Tree.*
Mishquáwtuck.	*The Cedar tree.*
Cówaw-ésuck.	*Pine-young Pine.*
Wenomesíppaguash.	*The Vine-Tree.*
Micúckaskeete.	*A Medow.*
Tataggoskituash.	*A fresh Medow.*
Maskituash.	*Grasse or Hay.*
Wékinash-quash.	*Reed, Reedes.*
Manisímmin.	*To cut or mow.*
Qussuckomineânug.	*The Cherry Tree.*
Wuttáhimneash.	*Strawberries.*

Obs. This Berry is the wonder of all the Fruits growing naturally in those parts: It is of it selfe Excellent: so that one of the chiefest Doctors of *England* was wont to say, that God could have made, but God never did make a better Berry: In some parts where the *Natives* have planted, I have many times seen as many as would filla good ship within few miles compasse: the *Indians* bruise them in a Morter, and mixe them with meale and make Strawberry·bread.

Wuchipoquáme-

| Wuchipoquáme- neash. | *A kind of sharp Fruit like a Barbary in tast.* |

Sasèmineash another sharp cooling Fruit growing in fresh Waters all the Winter, Excellent in conserve against Feavers.

Wenómeneash.	*Grapes.*
Wuttahimnasíppa- guash.	*Strawberry leaves.*
Peshaûiuash.	*Violet leaves.*
Nummoúwinneem.	*I goe to gather.*
Mowinne-aûog.	*He or they gather.*
Atáuntowash.	*Clime the Tree.*
Ntáuntawem.	*I clime.*
Punnoûwash.	*Come downe.*
Npunnowaûmen	*I come downe.*
Attitaash.	*Hurtle-berries.*

Of which there are divers sorts sweete like Currants, some opening, some of a binding nature.

Saūtaash are these Currants dried by the *Natives,* and so preserved all the yeare, which they beat to powder, and mingle it with their parcht meale, and make a delicate dish which they cal *Sautáuthig;* which is as sweet to them as plum or spice cake to the *English.*

They also make great use of their Strawberries having such abundance of them, making Strawberry bread, and having no other

H   Food

Food for many dayes, but the Ɛnglish have ex-
ceeded, and make good Wine both of their
Grapes and Strawberries also in some places,
as I have often tasted.

Ewáchim-neash.	*Corne.*
Scannémeneash.	*Seed-Corne.*
Wompiscannémene- ash.	*White seed-corne.*

Obs. There be diverse sorts of this Corne,
and of the colours: yet all of it either boild
in milke, or buttered, if the use of it were
knowne and received in *England* (it is the opinion of some skillfull in physick) it might
save many thousand lives in *England*, occasioned by the binding nature of *English* wheat,
the *Indian* Corne keeping the body ín a constant moderate loosenesse.

Aukeeteaûmen.	*To plant Corne.*
Quttáunemun.	*To plant Corne.*
Anakáusu.	*A Labourer.*
Anakáusichick.	*Labourers.*
Aukeeteaûmitch.	*Planting time.*
Aukeeteáhettit.	*When they set Corne.*
Nummautaukeeteaû- men.	*I have done planting.*
Anaskhómmin.	*To how or break up.*

Obs. The Women set or plant, weede, and
hill, and gather and barne all the corne, and
Fruites

Fruites of the field: Yet sometimes the man himselfe, (either out of love to his Wife, or care for his Children, or being an old man) will help the Woman which (by the custome of the Countrey) they are not bound to.

When a field is to be broken up, they have a very loving sociable speedy way to dispatch it: All the neighbours men and Women forty, fifty, a hundred &c, joyne, and come in to help freely.

With friendly joyning they breake up their fields, build their Forts, hunt the Woods, stop and kill fish in the Rivers, it being true with them as in all the World in the Affaires of Earth or Heaven: By concord little things grow great, by discord the greatest come to nothing *Concordiâ parvæ res crescunt, Discordiâ magnæ dilabuntur.*

Anáskhig-anash.	*How, Howes.*
Anaskhómwock.	*They how.*
Anaskhommonteâ-min.	*They break for me.*
Anaskhomwáutow-win.	*A breaking up How.*

The *Indian* Women to this day (notwithstanding our Howes, doe use their naturall Howes of shells and Wood.

Monaskún-

Monaskúnnemun.	*To weede.*
Monaskunnummaû-towwin.	*A weeding or broad How.*
Petascúnnemun,	*To hill the Corne.*
Kepenúmmin &* Wuttúnnemun.	*To gather Corne.*
Núnnowwa.	*Harvest time.*
Anoûant.	*At harvest.*
Wuttúnnemitch-Ewáchim.	*When harvest is in.*
Pausinnummin.	*To dry the corne.*

Which they doe carefully upon heapes and Mats many dayes, before they barne it up. covering it up with Mats at night, and opening when the Sun is hot.

Sókenug.	*A heap of corne.*

Obs. The woman of the family will commonly raise two or three heaps of twelve, fifteene, or twentie bushells a heap, which they drie in round broad heaps; and if she have helpe of her children or friends, much more.

Pockhómmin.	*To beat or thrash out.*
Npockhómmin.	*I am threshing.*
Cuppockhómmin?	*Doe you thrash?*
Wuskokkamuckóme-neash.	*New ground Corne.*
Nquitawánnanash.	*One basketfulll.*
Munnòte,-tash.	*Basket, Baskets.*

Mâúseck,

Máûseck.	*A great one*
Peewâsick.	*A little one.*
Wussaumepewâsick.	*Too little.*
Pokowánnanash.	*Halfe a basketfull.*
Neesowannanash.	*Two baskets full.*
Shóanash.	*Three.*
Yowanannash.	*Foure, &c.*
Aníttash.	*Rotten corne.*
Wawéekanash.	*Sweet corne.*
Tawhìtch quitche máuntamen?	*Why doe you smell to it?*
Auqúnnash.	*Barnes.*
Necawnaúquanash.	*Old barnes.*

Askútasquash, their Vine aples, which the *English* from them call *Squashes* about the bignesse of Apples of severall colours, a sweet, light wholesome refreshing.

Uppakumíneash.	*The seed of them.*

The Observation *Generall of the* Fruits *of the Earth.*

God hath not left himselfe without witin all parts and coasts of the world; the raines and fruitfull seasons, the Earth, Trees, Plants, &c. filling mans heart with food and gladnesse, witnesseth against, and condemneth man for his unthankfulnesse and unfruitfulnesse towards his Maker.

More particular:

Yeeres thousands since, God gaue command
  (as we in Scripture find)
That Earth *and* Trees *&* Plants *should bring*
  Forth fruits each in his kind.

The Wildernesse remembers this,
  The wild and howling land
Answers the toyling labour of,
  The wildest Indians *hand.*

But man forgets his Maker, *who,*
  Fram'd him in Righteousnesse.
A paradise in Paradise, now worse
  Then Indian *Wildernesse.*

CHAP. XVII.

Of *Beasts, &c.*

P Enashímwock. | *Beasts.*
  Netasûog. | *Cattell.*

Obs. This name the *Indians* give to tame Beasts, yea, and Birds also which they keepe tame about their houses:

Muck-

Muckquashim-wock.	*Wolves.*
Moattôqus.	*A blacke Wolfe.*
Tummòck quaûog Nóosup Súmhup. }paûog.	*Beaver, - Beavers.*

Obs. This is a Beast of wonder; for cutting and drawing of great pieces of trees with his teeth, with which, and sticks and earth I have often seen, faire streames and rivers damm'd and stopt up by them: upon these streames thus damm'd up, he builds his house with stories, wherein he sits drie in his chambers, or goes into the water at his pleasure.

Mishquáshim.	*A red Fox.*
Péquawus.	*A gray Fox.*

Obs. The *Indians* say they have black Foxes, which they have often seene, but never could take any of them: they say they are *Manittóoes,* that is, Gods Spirits or Divine powers, as they say of every thing which they cannot comprehend.

Aûsup-pánnog.	*Racoone, Racoones*
Nkèke, nkéquock.	*Otter, Otters.*
Pussoûgh.	*The wildcat.*

Ockgutchaun-nng. A wild beast of a reddish haire about the bignesse of a *Pig,* and rooting like a *Pig;* from whence they give this name to all our *Swine.*   H 4   Mishan-

Mishánneke-quock.	*Squirrill, quirrils.*
Anéqusanéquussuck.	*A litle coloured Squirril.*
Waûtuckques.	*The Conie.*

Obs. They have a reverend esteeme of this Creature, and conceive there is some Deitie in it.

Attuck, quock.	
Nóonatch noónat- 　　chaug.	}*Deere.*
Moósquin.	*A Fawn.*
Wawwúnnes.	*A young Bucke.*
Kuttíomp & Paucot- 　　tâuwaw.	*A great Bucke.*
Aunàn-quunèke.	*A Doe.*
Qunnequáwese.	*A little young Doe.*
Naynayoûmewot.	*A Horse.*
Côwsnuck.	*Cowes.*
Gôatesuck.	*Goats.*
Hógsuck. Pígsuck.	*Swine.*

Obs. This Termination *suck*, is common in their language; and therefore they adde it to our *English* Cattell, not else knowing what names to give them;

Anùm.	*A Dog.*

Yet the varietie of their Dialects and proper speech within thirtie or fortie miles each of
other,

other, is very great, as appeares in that word,

Anùm,	The *Cowweset*
Ayím,	The *Narriganset*
Arúm.	The *Qunnippiuck*
Alùm.	The *Neepmuck*

} Dialect.

So that although some pronounce not *L*, nor *R*. yet it is the most proper Dialect of other places, contrary to many reports.

Enewáshim.	*A Male.*
Squáshim.	*A Female.*
Moòs sóog.	*The great Oxe, or rather a red Deere.*
Askùg.	*A Snake.*
Móaskug.	*Black Snake.*
Sések.	*Rattle Snake.*
Natúppwock.	*They feed.*
Téaqua natuphéttit?	*What shall they eat?*
Natuphéttitch yo fanáukamick.	*Let them feed on this ground.*

The generall Observation *of the Beasts.*

The Wildernesse is a cleere resemblance of the world, where greedie and furious men persecute and devoure the harmlesse and innocent as the wilde beasts pursue and devoure the Hinds and Roes.

More

More particular.

1. *The* Indians, *Wolves, yea, Dogs and Swine,*
I have knowne the Deere devoure,
Gods children are sweet prey to all;
But yet the end proves sowre.

2 *For though Gods children lose their lives,*
They shall not loose an haire;
But shall arise, and judge all those,
That now their Iudges are.

3 New-England's *wilde beasts are not fierce,*
As other wild beasts are:
Some men are not so fierce, and yet
From mildnesse are they farre.

Chap. XVIII.

Of *the Sea.*

WEchêkum Kítthan. }	*The Sea.*
Paumpágussit.	*The Sea-God,* or, that

name which they give that Deitie or God-
head which they conceive to be in the Sea.

Obs. Mishoòn an *Indian* Boat, or Canow
made of a Pine or Oake, or Chestnut-tree: I
have seene a Native goe into the woods with
his hatchet, carrying onely a Basket of Corne
with

with him, & stones to strike fire when he had
feld his tree (being a *chesnut*) he made him a
little House or shed of the bark of it, he puts
fire and followes the burning of it with fire, in
the midst in many places: his corne he boyles
and hath the Brook by him, and sometimes
angles for a little fish; but so hee continues
burning and hewing untill he hath within ten
or twelve dayes (lying there at his worke a-
lone) finished, and (getting hands,) lanched
his Boate; with which afterward hee ventures out to fish in the Ocean.

| Mishoonémese. | *A little Canow.* |

Some of them will not well carry above
three or foure: but some of them twenty,
thirty, forty men.

| Wunnauanoûnuck. | *A Shallop.* |
| Wunnauanounuck-
quèse. | *A Skiffe.* |

Obs. Although themselves have neither,
yet they give them such names, which in
their Language signifieth carrying Vessells.

Kitônuck.	*A Ship.*
Kitónuckquese.	*A little ship.*
Mishíttouwand.	*A great Canow.*
Peewàsu.	*A little one.*
Paugautemissaûnd.	*An Oake Canow.*

Kowwow-

Kowawwaûnd.	*A pine Canow.*
Wompmissaûnd.	*A chesnut Canow.*
Ogwhan.	*A boat adrift.*
Wuskon-tógwhan.	*It will goe a drift.*
Cuttunnamíinnea.	*Help me to launch.*
Cuttunnummútta.	*Let us launch.*
Cuttúnnamoke.	*Launch.*
Cuttánnummous.	*I will help you.*
Wútkunck.	*A paddle or Oare.*
Namacóuhe cómishoon.	*Lend me your Boate.*
Paûtousnenótehunck	*Bring hither my paddle.*
Comishoónhom?	*Goe you by water?*
Chémosh-chémeck.	*Paddle or row.*
Maumínikish & Maumanetepweéas.	*Pull up, or row lustily.*
Sepâkehig.	*A Sayle.*
Sepagehommaûta.	*Let us saile.*
Wunnâgehan.	*We have a faire wind.*

Obs. Their owne reason hath taught them, to pull of a Coat or two and set it up on a small pole, with which they will saile before a wind ten, or twenty mile, &c.

Wauaúpunish.	*Hoyse up.*
Wuttáutnish.	*Pull to you.*
Nókanish.	*Take it downe.*
Pakétenish.	*Let goe or let flie.*
Nikkoshkowwaûmen.	*We shall be drown'd.*

Nquawup-

Nquawu pshâwmen.	*We overset.*
Wussaûme peche-paûsha.	*The Sea comes in too fast upon us.*
Maumaneeteántass.	*Be of good courage.*

Obs. It is wonderfull to see how they will venture in those Canoes, and how (being oft overset as I have my selfe been with them) they will swim a mile, yea two or more safe to Land: I having been necessitated to passe waters diverse times with them, it hath pleased God to make them many times the instruments of my preservation: and when sometimes in great danger I have questioned safety, they have said to me: Feare not, if we be overset I will carry you safe to Land.

Paupaútuckquash.	*Hold water.*
Kínnequass.	*Steere.*
Tiáckomme kínni-quass.	*Steere right.*
Kunnósnep.	*A Killick, or Anchor.*
Chowwophómmin.	*To cast over-boord.*
Chouwóphash.	*Cast over-board*
Touwopskhómmke.	*Cast anchor.*
Mishittashin.	*It is a storme.*
Awêpesha.	*It caulmes.*
Awêpu.	*A calme.*
Nanoúwashin.	*A great caulme.*
Tamóccon.	*Floud.*

Nanashowetamóccon	*Halfe Floud.*
Keesaqúshin.	*High water.*
Taumacoks.	*Vpon the Floud.*
Mishittommóckon.	*A great Floud.*
Maúchetan & skàt.	*Ebb.*
Mittâeskat.	*A low Ebb.*
Awánick Paûdhuck?	*Who comes there?*

Obs. I have knowne thirty or forty of their Canowes fill'd with men, and neere as many more of their enemies in a Sea-fight.

Caupaúshess.	*Goe ashoare.*
Caupaushâuta.	*Let us goe ashoare.*
Wusséheposh.	*Heave out the water.*
Asképunish.	*Make fast the Boat.*
Kspúnsh & Kspúne- moke.	*Tie it fast.*
Maumínikish.	*Tie it hard.*
Neene Cuthómwock.	*Now they goe off.*
Kekuthomwushán- nick.	*They are gone already.*

Generall Observations *of the* Sea.

How unsearchable are the depth of the Wisedome and Power of God in separating from *Europe*, *Asia* and *Africa* such a mightie vast continent as *America* is? and that for so

many

many ages? as also, by such a Westerne Ocean of about three thousand of *English* miles
breadth in passage over?

> More particular:
> *They see Gods wonders that are call'd*
> *Through dreadfull Seas to passe,*
> *In tearing winds and roaring seas,*
> *And calmes as smooth as glasse.*
> *I have in* Europes *ships, oft been*
> *In King of terrours hand;*
> *When all have cri'd,* Now, now we sinck,
> *Yet God bronght safe to land.*
> *Alone 'mongst* Indians *in Canoes,*
> *Sometimes o're-turn'd, I have been*
> *Halfe inch from death, in Ocean deepe,*
> *Gods wonders I have seene.*

Chap. XIX.

Of *Fish* and *Fishing*.

NAmaùs,-suck.
Pauganaùt,tam-
wock.
fore the Spring.

Fish, Fishes.
Cod, Which is the first
that comes a little be-

Qunna-

Qunnamáug-suck. | *Lampries.* The first
that come in the Spring into the fresh Rivers.

Aumsûog, *&* Munna- | *A Fish somewhat like*
    whatteaûg. | *a Herring.*

Missúckeke-kéquock. | *Basse.* The *Indians*
(and the *English* too) make a daintie dish of
the *Uppaquóntup,* or head of this Fish; and
well they may, the braines and fat of it being very much, and sweet as marrow.

Kaúposh-shaûog. | *Sturgeon.*

Obs. Divers part of the Countrey abound
with this Fish; yet the Natives for the goodnesse and greatnesse of it, much prize it and
will neither furnish the *English* with so many,
nor so cheape, that any great trade is like to
be made of it, untill the *English* themselves are
fit to follow the fishing.

The Natives venture one or two in a Canow, and with an harping Iron, or such like
Instrument sticke this fish, and so hale it into
their Canow; sometimes they take them by
their nets, which they make strong of Hemp.

Ashòp. | *Their Nets.* Which
they will set thwart some little River or Cove
wherein they kil Basse (at the fall of the water)
with their arrows, or sharp sticks, especially if
headed with Iron, gotten from the *Engish,* &c.

                                  Aucup.

Aucup	*A little Cove or Creeke.*
Aucppâwese.	*A very little one.*
Wawwhunnekesûog.	*Mackrell.*
Mishquammauquock.	*Red fish, Salmon.*
Osacóntuck.	*A fat sweet fish,* something like a *Haddock.*
Mishcùp-paûog, Sequanamauquock.	*Breame.*

Obs. Of this fish there is abundance which the Natives drie in the Sunne and smoake; and some *English* begin to salt, both wayes they keepe all the yeere; and it is hoped it may be as well accepted as Cod at a Market, and better, if once knowne.

Taut-auog.	*Sheeps-heads.*
Neeshaûog Sassammauquock Nquittéconnaúog	*Eeles.*
Tatackommmàuog.	*Porpuses.*
Pótop-pauog.	*Whales:* Which in

some places are often cast up; I have seene some of them, but not above sixtie foot long: The *Natives* cut them out in severall parcells, and give and send farre and neere for an acceptable present, or dish.

Missêsu.	*The whole.*
Poquêsu.	*The halfe.*
Waskèke.	*The Whalebone.*

I

Wufsúck-

Wussúckqun.	*A taile.*
Aumaũog.	*They are fishing.*
Ntaûmen.	*I am fishing.*
Kuttaũmen?	*Doe you fish?*
Nnattuckqunnúwem.	*I goe afishing.*
Aumáchick,	
Natuckqunnuwâ-chick.	*Fishes.*
Aumaûi.	*He is gone to fish.*
Awácenick kukkatti-neanaûmen?	*What doe you fish for?*
Ashaũnt-teaũg.	*Lobsters*
Opponenaũhock.	*Oysters.*
Sickìssuog.	*Clams.*

Obs. This is a sweet kind of shelfish, which all *Indians* generally over the Countrey, Winter and Summer delight in; and at low water the women dig for them: this fish, and the naturall liquor of it, they boile, and it makes their broth and their *Nasaũmp* (which is a kind of thickned broth) and their bread seasonable and savory, instead of Salt: and for that the *English* Swine dig and root these Clams wheresoever they come, and watch the low water (as the *Indian* women do) therefore of all the *Euglish* Cattell, the Swine (as also because of their filthy disposition) are

most

most hatefull to all Natives, and they call them filthy cut throats &c.

Séqunnock.	*A Horse-fish.*
Poquaûhock.	

Obs. This the English call Hens, a little thick shel-fiish, which the Indians wade deepe and dive for, and after they have eaten the meat there (in those which are good) they breake out of the shell, about halfe an inch of a blacke part of it, of which they make their *Suckaûhock*, or black money, which is to them pretious.

Meteaûhock. | *The Periwinckle.* Of which they make their *Wòmpans*, or white money, of halfe the value of their *Suckáwhock*, or blacke money, of which more in the Chapter of their Coyne.

Cumménakiss,	
Cummenak ssamen	*Have you taken store?*
Cummuchickinnea- nâwmen?	
Numménakiss.	*I have taken store.*
Nummuchikinea- nâwmen.	*I have killed many.*
Machàge.	*I have caught none.*
Aúmanep,	*A fishing-line.*
Aumanápeash.	*Lines.*

The Natives take exceeding great paines in their fishing, especially in watching their seasons by night; so that frequently they lay their naked bodies many a cold night on the cold shoare about a fire of two or three sticks, and oft in the night search their Nets; and sometimes goe in and stay longer in frozen water.

Hoquaùn aûnash.	*Hooke, hookes.*
Peewâsicks.	*Little hookes.*
Maúmacocks.	*Great hookes.*
Nponamouôog.	*I set nets for them.*
Npunnouwaûmen.	*I goe to search my nets.*
Mihtúck quashep.	*An Eele-pot.*
Kunnagqunneûteg.	*A greater sort.*
Onawangónnakaun.	*A baite.*
Yo onawangónnatees	*Baite with this.*
Moamitteaŭg.	*A little sort of fish,*

halfe as big as Sprats, plentifull in Winter.

Paponaumsũog. | *A winter fish,* which comes up in the brookes and rivulets; some call them Frost fish, from their comming up from the Sea into fresh Brookes, in times of frost and snow.

Qunôsuog. | *A fresh fish;* which the *Indians* break the Ice in fresh ponds, when they take also many other sorts: for, to my know-ledge the Country yeelds many sorts of other fish, which I mention not.   *The*

The generall Observation *of Fish.*

How many thousands of Millions of those under water, sea-Inhabitants, in all Coasts of the world preach to the sonnes of men on shore, to adore their glorious Maker by presenting themselves to Him as themselves (in a manner) present their lives from the wild Ocean, to the very doores of men, their fellow creatures in *New England.*

More Particular.

What Habacuck *once spake, mine eyes*
   Have often seene most true,
The greater fishes devoure the lesse,
   And cruelly pursue.

Forcing them though Coves and Creekes,
   To leape on driest sand,
To gaspe on earthie element, or die
   By wildest Indians *hand.*

Christs little ones must hunted be
   Devour'd; yet rise as Hee.
And eate up those which now a while
   Their fierce devourers be.

Chap. XX.

Of *their nakednesse* and *clothing*.

Paūskesu.	*Naked.*
Pauskesítchick	*Naked men and women.*
Nippóskiss.	*I am naked.*

They have a two-fold nakednesse:

First ordinary and constant, when although they have a Beasts skin, or an English mantle on, yet that covers ordinarily but their hinder parts and all the foreparts from top to toe, (excep their secret parts, covered with a little Apron, after the patterne of their and our first Parents) I say all else open and naked.

Their male children goe starke naked, and have no Apron untill they come to ten or twelve yeeres of age; their Female they, in a modest blush cover with a little Apron of an hand breadth from their very birth.

Their second nakednesse is when their men often abroad, and both men and women within doores, leave off their beasts skin, or English cloth and so (excepting their little Apron) are wholly naked; yet but few of the women but will keepe their skin or cloth (though loose)

loose) or neare to them ready to gather it up about them.

Custome hath used their minds and bodies to it, and in such a freedom from any wantonnesse, that I have never seen that wantonnesse amongst them, as, (with griefe) I have heard of in *Europe.*

Nippóskenitch.	*I am rob'd of my coat.*
Nippóskenick ewò.	*He takes away my Coat.*
Acòh.	*Their Deere skin.*
Tummóckquashunck.	*A Beavers coat.*
Nkéquashunck.	*An Otters coat.*
Mohéwonck.	*A Rakoone-skin coat.*
Natóquashunck.	*A Wolues-skin coat.*
Mishannéquashunck.	*A Squirrill-skin coat.*
Neyhommaûashunck	A *Coat or Manlte,* cu-

riously made of the fairest feathers of their *Neyhommaûog,* or Turkies, which commonly their old men make; and is with them as Velvet with us.

Maũnek: nquittiashí-agat.	*An English Coat or Mantell.*
Cáudnish.	*Put off.*
Ocquash.	*Put on.*
Neesashíagat.	*Two coats.*
Shwíshiagat.	*Three coats.*
Piuckquashíagat.	*Ten coats, &c.*

Obs. Within their skin or coat they creepe

contentedly, by day or night, in house, or in
the woods, and sleep soundly counting it a fe-
lícitie, (as indeed an earthly one it *is*; *Intra
pelliculam quen,que teneresuam*, That every
man be content with his skin.

Squáus aúhaqut.	*a Womans Mantle.*
Muckíis auhaqut.	A *childs Mantle.*
Pétacaus.	*an English Wastecoat.*
Petacawsunnèse.	*a little wastecoat.*
Aũtah & aútawhun.	*Their apron.*
Caukóanash.	*Stockins.*
Nquittetiagáttash.	*a paire of stockins.*
Mocússinass, & Mockussínchass.	*Shooes.*

Obs. Both these, Shoes and Stockins they
make of their Deerc skin worne out, which
yet being excellently tann'd by them is excellent for to travell in wet and snow; for it
is so well tempered with oyle, that the water
cleane wrings out; and being hang'd up in
their chimney, they presently drie without
hurt as my selfe hath often proved.

Noonacóminash.	*Too little.*
Taubacóminash.	*Big enough.*
Saunketíppo, *or,* Ashónaquo.	*a Hat or Cap.*
Moôse.	*The skin of a great Beast*

as big as an Ox, some call it a red Deere.

Wussuck-

Wussuckhósu. | *Painted.*

They also commonly paint these *Moose* and Deere-skins for their Summer wearing, with varietie of formes and colours.

Petouwássinug. | *Their Tobacco-bag,* which hangs at their necke, or sticks at their girdle, which is to them in stead of an English pocket.

Obs. Our English clothes are so strange unto them, and their bodies inured so to indure the weather, that when (upon gift &c.) some of them have had *English* cloathes, yet in a showre of raine, I have seen them rather expose their skins to the wet then their cloaths, and therefore pull them off, and keep them drie.

Obs. While they are amongst the *English* they keep on the *English* apparell, but pull of all, as soone as they come againe into their owne Houses, and Company.

Generall Observations *of their Garments.*

How deep are the purposes and Councells, of God? what should bee the reason of this mighty difference of One mans children that all the Sonnes of men on this side the way (in *Europe,* *Asia* and *Africa* should have such plenteous clothing for Body for Soule! and the rest of *Adams* sonnes and Daughters on
                                                        the

the other side, or *America* (some thinke as
big as the other three,) should neither have
nor desire clothing for their naked Soules, or
Bodies.

More particular:

O what a Tyrant's Custome long,
  How doe men make a tush,
At what's in use, though ne're so fowle:
  Without once shame or blush?

Many thousand proper Men and Women,
  I have seen met in one place:
Almost all naked, yet not one,
  Thought want of clothes disgrace.

Israell was naked, wearing cloathes! } Exod.
  The best clad English-man,   }
Not cloth'd with Christ, more naked is: } 32.
  Then naked Indian.

Chap. XXI.

Of Religion, the soule, &c.

M Anìt-manittó. | *God, Gods.*
  wock. |

                                    Obs.

Obs. He that questions whether God made the World, the *Indians* will teach him. I must acknowledge I have received in my converse with them many Confirmations of those two great points, *Heb.* II. 6. *viz:*

1. That God is.

2. That hee is a rewarder of all them that diligently seek him.

They will generally confesse that God made all: but then in speciall, although they deny not that *English-mans* God made *English* Men, and the heavens and Earth there! yet their Gods made them and the Heaven, and Earth where they dwell.

Nummusquauna-múckqun manìt.	*God is angry with me?*

Obs. I have heard a poore *Indian* lamenting the losse of a child at break of day, call up his Wife and children, and all about him to Lamentation, and with abundance of teares cry out! O God thou hast taken away my child! thou art angry with me: O turne thine anger from me, and spare the rest of my children.

If they receive any good in hunting, fishing, Harvest &c. they acknowledge God in it.

Yea, if it be but an ordinary accident, a fall, &c. they will say God was angry and did it,

mus-

musquàntum manit God is angry. But herein
is their Misery.

First they branch their God-head into many Gods.

Secondly, attribute it to Creatures.

First, many Gods: they have given me
the Names of thirty seven which I have, all
which in their solemne Worships they invocate: as

Kautántowwìt the great *South-West* God, to
to whose House all soules goe, and from
whom came their Corne, Beanes, as they say.

Wompanand.	*The Easterne God.*
Chekesuwànd.	*The Westerne God.*
Wunnanaméanit.	*The Northerne God.*
Sowwanànd.	*The Southerne God.*
Wetuómanit.	*The house God.*

Even as the Papists have their He and Shee
Saint Protectors as St. *George,* St. *Patrick,*
St. *Denis,* Virgin *Mary,* &c.

Squáuanit.	*The Womans God.*
Muckquachuck- quànd.	*The Childrens God,*

Obs. I was once with a *Native* dying of a
wound, given him by some murtherous *English* (who rob'd him and run him through
with a Rapier, from whom in the heat of his
wound, he at present escaped from them, but
dying

dying of his wound, they suffered Death at new *Plymouth*, in *New-England*, this *Native* dying call'd much upon *Muckquachuckquànd*, which of other *Natives* I understood (as they believed) had appeared to the dying young man, many yeares before, and bid him when ever he was in distresse call upon him.

Secondly, as they have many of these fained Deities: so worship they the Creatures in whom they conceive doth rest some Deitie:

Keesuckquànd.	*The Sun God.*
Nanepaûshat.	*The Moone God.*
Paumpágussit.	*The Sea.*
Yotáanit.	*The Fire God,*

Supposing that Deities be in these, &c.

When I have argued with them about their Fire-God: can it say they be but this fire must be a God, or Divine power, that out of a stone will arise in a Sparke and when a poore naked *Indian* is ready to starve with cold in the House, and especially in the Woods, often saves his life, doth dresse all our Food for us, and if it be angry will burne the House about us, yea if a spark fall into the drie wood, burnes up the Country, (though this burning of the Wood to them they count a benefit,

Benefit both for destroying of vermin, and keeping downe the Weeds and thickets?)

Presentem narrat quælibet herba Deum.
Every little Grasse doth tell,
The sons of Men, there God doth dwell.

Besides there is a generall Custome amongst them, at the apprehension of any Excellency in Men, Women, Birds Beasts, Fish, &c. to cry out *Manittóo*, that is, it is a God, as thus if they see one man excell others in Wisdome, Valour, strength, Activity &c. they cry out *Manittóo* A God: and therefore when they talke amongst themselves of the *English* ships, and great buildings, of the plowing of their Fields, and especially of Bookes and Letters, they will end thus: *Manittôwock* They are Gods: *Cummanittôo*, you are a God, &c. A strong Conviction naturall in the soule of man, that God is; filling all things, and places, and that all Excellencies dwell in God, and proceed from him, and that they only are blessed who have that Jehovah their portion.

Nickómmo. | *A Feast or Dance.*

Of this Feast they have publike, and private and that of two sorts.

First in sicknesse, or Drouth, or Warre or Famine.   Secondly,

Secondly, After Harvest, after hunting, when they enjoy a caulme of Peace, Health, Plenty, Prosperity, then *Nickómmo* a Feast, especially in Winter, for then (as the Turke faith of the Christian, rather the Antichristian,) they run mad once a yeare) in their kind of Christmas feasting.

| Powwaw. | *A Priest.* |
| Powwaûog. | *Priests.* |

Obs. These doe begin and order their service, and Invocation of their Gods, and all the people follow, and joyne interchangeably in a laborious bodily service, unto sweatings, especially of the Priest, who spends himselfe in strange Antick Gestures, and Actions even unto fainting.

In sicknesse the Priest comes close to the sick person, and performes many strange Actions about him, aud threaten and conjures out the sicknesse. They conceive that there are many Gods or divine Powers within the body of a man: In his pulse, his heart, his Lungs, &c.

I confesse to have most of these their customes by their owne Relation, for after once being in their Houses and beholding what their Worship was, I durst never bee an eye witnesse, Spectatour, or looker on, least I

should

should have been partaker of Sathans Inventions and Worships, contrary to *Ephes.* 5, 14.

Nanouwétea.	*An over-Seer and Or-*
	derer of their Worship.
Neen nanowwúnne-	*I will order or*
mun.	*oversee.*

They have an exact forme of King, Priest,
and Prophet, as was in Israel typicall of old
in that holy Land of *Canaan,* and as the Lord
Iesus ordained in his spirituall Land of *Canaan*
his Church throughout the whole World:
their Kings or Governours called *Sachimaüog,*
Kings, and *Atauskowaŭg* Rulers doe govern:
Their Priests, performe and manage their
Worship: Their wise men and old men of
which number the Priests are also,) whom
they call *Taupowaüog* they make solemne
speeches and Orations, or Lectures to them,
concerning Religion, Peace, or Warre and all
things.

Nowemaúsitteem.| *I give away at the Worship.*

He or she that makes this *Nickòmmo* Feast
or Dance, besides the *F*easting of sometimes
twenty, fifty, and hundreth, yea I have seene
neere a thousand persons at one of these
Feasts) they give I say a great quantity of
money, and all sort of their goods (according to and sometimes beyond their Estate)

In

in severall small parcells of goods, or money, to the value of eighteen pence, two Shillings, or thereabouts to one person: and that person that receives this Gift, upon the receiving of it goes out, and hollowes thrice for the health and prosperity of the Party that gave it, the Mr. or Mistris of the Feast.

Nowemacaúnash.	*Ile give these things.*
Nitteaúguash.	*My money.*
Nummaumachíuwash.	*My goods.*

Obs. By this Feasting and Gifts, the Divell drives on their worships pleasantly (as he doth all false worships, by such plausible Earthly Arguments of uniformities, universalities, Antiquities, Immunities, Dignities, Rewards, unto submitters, and the contrary to Refusers) so that they run farre and neere and aske

Awaun. Nákommit ?	*Who makes a Feast?*
Nkekinneawaûmen.	*I goe to the Feast.*
Kekineawaûi.	*He is gone to the Feast.*

They have a modest Religious perswasion not to disturb any man, either themselves *English, Dutch,* or any in their Conscience, and worship, and therefore say:

Aquiewopwaûwash.	*Peace, hold your peace.*
Aquiewopwaûwock.	

K | Peeyaúntam.

Peeyáuntam.	*He is at Prayer*.
Peeyaúntamwock.	*They are praying*.
Cowwéwonck.	*The Soule*,

Derived from *Cowwene* to sleep, because say they, it workes and operates when the body sleepes. *Míchachunck* the soule, in a higher notion which is of affinity, with a word signifying a looking glasse, or cleere resemblance, so that it hath its name from a cleere sight or discerning, which indeed seemes very well to suit with the nature of it.

Wuhóck.	*The Body*
Nohòck: cohòck.	*My body, your body*.
Awaunkeesitteoúwin- cohòck:	*Who made you?*
Tunna-awwa com- mítchichunck- kitonckquèan?	*Whether goes your soule when you die?*
An. Sowánakit- aúwaw.	*It goes to the South-West*.

Obs. They believe that the soules of Men and Women goe to the Sou-west, their great and good men and Women to *Cautàntouwit* his House, where they have hopes (as the Turkes have of carnall Joyes): Murtherers thieves and Lyers, their Soules (say they) wander restlesse abroad.

Now because this Book (by Gods good providence)

vidence) may come into the hand of many
fearing God, who may also have many an opportunity of occasionall discourse with some
of these their wild brethren and Sisters, and
may speake a word for their and our glorious
Maker, which may also prove some prepara-
tory Mercy to their Soules: I shall propose
some proper expressions concerning the Creation of the World, and mans Estate, and in
particular theirs also, which from my selfe
many hundreths of times, great numbers of
them have heard with great delight, and
great convictions: which who knowes (in
Gods holy season) may rise to the exalting
of the Lord Jesus Christ in their conversion,
and salvation.

Nétop Kunnatóte-mous.	*Friend, I will aske you a Question.*
Natótema:	*Speake on.*
Tocketunnântum?	*What thinke you?*
Awaun Keesiteoû-win Kéesuck?	*Who made the Heavens?*
Aûke Wechêkom?	*The Earth, the Sea?*
Míttauke.	*The World.*

Some will answer *Tattá* I cannot tell, some
will answer *Manittôwock* the Gods.

Tà suóg Manítto-wock.	*How many Gods bee there?*

Maunaûog-

Maunaŭog Mishaú-nawock.	*Many, great many.*
Nétop machàge.	*Friend, not so.*
Paŭsuck naŭnt manìt.	*There is onely one God.*
Cuppíssittone.	*You are mistaken.*
Cowauwaúnemun.	*You are out of the way.*

A phrase which much pleaseth them, being proper for their wandring in the woods, and similitudes greatly please them.

Kukkakótemous, wâ-chit-quáshouwe.	*I will tell you, presently.*
Kuttaunchemókous.	*I will tell you newes.*
Paŭsuck naŭnt maníť kéesittin keesuck, &c	*One onely God made the Heavens, &c.*
Napannetashèmittan naugecautúmmo-nab nshque.	*Five thousand yeers agoe and upwards.*
Naŭgom naŭnt wuk-kesittínnes wâme teâgun.	*He alone made allthings*
Wuche mateâg.	*Out of nothing.*
Quttatashuchuckqún-nacaus-keesitínnes wâme.	*In six dayes he made all things.*
Nquittaqúnne. Wuckéesitin wequâi.	*The first day Hee made the Light.*
Néesqunne. Wuckéesitin Keésuck.	*The second day Hee made the Firmameut.*
	Shúck

Shúckqunne wuckée-sitin Aūke kà wechêkom.	*The third day hee made the Earth and Sea.*
Yóqunne wuckkéesi-tin Nippaūus kà Nanepaūshat.	*The fourth day he made the Sun and the Moon.*
Neenash-mamockíu-wash wêquanantí-ganash.	*Two great Lights.*
Kà wáme anócksuck.	*And all the Starres.*
Napannetashúck-qunne Wuckéesittin pussuckseésuck wâme.	*The fifth day hee made all the Fowle.*
Keesuckquíuke.	*In the Ayre, or Heavens.*
Ka wáme namaūsuck. Wechekommíuke.	*And all the Fish in the Sea.*
Quttatashúkqunne wuckkeésittin pena-shímwock wamè.	*The sixth day hee made all the Beasts of the Field.*
Wuttàke wuchè wuckeesittin pau-suck Enìn, *or,* Enes-kéetomp.	*Last of all he made one Man*
Wuche mishquòck.	*Of red Earth,*
Ka wesuonckgonna-kaūnes Adam, túp-pautea mishquòck.	*And call'd him Adam, or red Earth,*

K 3   Wuttàke

Wuttàke wuchè,	*Then afteward, while Adam,* or *red Earth slept.*
Câwit míshquock.	
Wuckaudnúmmenes manìt peetaūgon wuche Adam.	*God tooke a rib from Adam,* or *red Earth.*
Kà wuchè peteaúgon.	*And of that rib he made One woman,*
Wukkeesitínnes paū-suck squàw.	
Kà pawtouwúnnes Adâmuck.	*And brought her to Adam.*
Nawônt Adam wut-túnnawaun nuppe-teâgon ewò.	*When Adam saw her, he said, This is my bone.*
Enadatashúckqunne, aquêi,	*The seventh day hee rested,*
Nagaû wuchè qutta-tashúckqune ana-caūsuock English-mánuck.	*And therefore English-men worke six dayes.*
Enadatashuckqun-nóckat taubataūm-wock.	*On the seventh day they praise God.*

Obs. At this Relation they are much sa-tisfied, with a reason why (as they observe) the *English* and *Dutch*, &c, labour six dayes, aud rest and worship the seventh.

Besides, they will say, Wee never heard of
this

this before: and then will relate how they have it from their Fathers, that *Kautántowwit* made one man and woman of a stone, which disliking, he broke them in pieces, and made another man and woman of a Tree, which were the Fountaines of all mankind.

They apprehending a vast difference of Knowledge betweene the *English* and themselves, are very observant of the *English* lives: I have heard them say to an Englishman (who being hindred, broke a promise to them) You know God, Will you lie Englishman?

Nétop kíhkita.	*Hearken to mee.*
Englishmánnuck,	*English men.*
Dutchmánnuck, kéenouwin kà wamè mittaukêukkitonck quéhettit.	*Dutch men, and you and all the world, when they die.*
Mattùx swowánna kit aûog, Michichónckquock.	*Their soules goe not to the Southwest.*
Wàme, ewò pâwsuck Manìt wawóntakick.	*All that know that one God.*
Ewò manìt waumaû sachick kà uckqushanchick.	*That love and feare Him.*
Keésaqut aùog.	*They goe up to Heaven.*

K 4   Michéme

Michéme weetean-támwock.	*They ever live in joy.*
Naûgom manìt wê-kick.	*In Gods owne House.*
Ewo manìt mat wau-óntakick.	*They that know not this God.*
Matwaumaûsachick.	*That love.*
Màt ewò uckqushán-chick.	*And feare him not.*
Kamóotakick.	*Thieves.*
Pupannouwâchick.	*Lyers.*
Nochisquauónchick.	*Vncleane persons.*
Nanompaníssichick,	*Idle persons.*
Kemineíachick.	*Murtherers.*
Mammaúsachick	*Adulterers.*
Nanisquégachick.	*Oppressors or fierce.*
Wame naûmaki-aûog.	*They goe to Hell or the Deepe.*
Micheme maûog.	*They shall ever lament.*
Awaun kukkakote-mógwunnes?	*Who told you so?*
Manittóo wússuck-wheke.	*Gods Booke or Writing.*

Obs. After I had (as farre as my language would reach) discoursed (upon a time) before the chiefe *Sachim* or *Prince* of the Countrey, with his *Archpriests*, and many other in a full Assembly; and being night, wearied with
                                    travell;

travell and discourse, I lay downe to rest; and before I slept, I heard this passage:

A *Qunníhticut* Indian (who had heard our discourse) told the *Sachim Miantunnōmu,* that soules went up to Heaven, or downe to Hell; For, saith he, Our fathers have told us, that our soules goe to the *Southwest.*

The *Sachim* answered, But how doe you know your selfe, that your soules goe to the *Southwest;* did you ever see a soule goe thither?

The Natiue replyed; when did he (naming my selfe) see a soule goe to Heaven or Hell?

The *Sachim* againe replied: He hath books and writings, and one which God himselfe made, concerning mens soules, and therefore may well know more than wee that have none, but take all upon trust from our forefathers.

The said *Sachim,* and the chiefe of his people, discoursed by themselves, of keeping the Englishmans day of worship, which I could easily have brought the Countrey to, but that I was perswaded, and am, that Gods way is first to turne a soule from it's Idolls, both of heart, worship, and conversation, before it is capable of worship, to the true and living God, according to *I Thes.* 1. 9. You turned
to

to God from Idolls to serve or worship the
living and true God. As also, that the two
first Principles and Foundations of true Religion or Worship of the true God in Christ,
are Repentance from dead workes, and Faith
towards God, before the Doctrine of Baptisme or washing and the laying on of hands,
which containe the Ordinances and Practices
of worship; the want of which, I conceive, is
the bane of million of soules in England, and
all other Nations professing to be Christian
Nations, who are brought by publique autho-
rity to Baptisme and fellowship with God in
Ordinances of worship, beforc the saving
worke of Repentance, and a true turning to
God, *Heb. 6. 2.*

Nétop, kitonckquêan kunnúppamin mi-chéme.	*Friend, when you die you perish everlast-ingly.*
Michéme cuppauqua neímmin.	*You are everlastingly undone.*
Cummusquauna múckqun manìt.	*God is angry with you.*
Cuppauquanúckqun	*He will destroy you.*
Wuchè cummanittó-wockmanâuog.	*For your many Gods.*

Wáme

| Wáme pìtch chíckau- ta mittaùke. | *The whole world shall ere long be bnrnt.* |

Obs. Upon the relating that God hath once destroyed the world by water; and that He will visit it the second time with consuming fire: I have been asked this profitable questi- on of some of them, What then will become of us? Where then shall we be?

| Manìt ánawat, Cuppittakúnnamun wèpe wáme. | *God commandth, That all men now re- pent.* |

The generall Observation *of* Religion, *&c.*

The wandring Generations of *Adams* lost posteritie, having lost the true and living God their Maker, have created out of the nothing of their owne inventions many false and fain- ed Gods and Creators.

More particular:

Two sorts of men shall naked stand.
  Before the burning ire   2 Thes. 1. 8.
Of him that shortly shall appeare,
  In dreadfull flaming fire.
First, millions know not God, nor for
  His *knowledge, care to seeke:*

Millions

Millions have knowledge store, but in
    Obedience are not meeke.
If woe to Indians, *Where shall* Turk,
    Where shall appeare the Iew?
O, where shall stand the Christian false?
    O blessed then the True.

Chap. XXII.

Of *their Government* and *Justice*.

Sâchim-maûog.	*King, Kings.*
Sachimaûonck,	*A Kingdome* or *Monarchie.*

Obs. Their Government is Monarchicall, yet at present the chiefest government in the Counrey is divided betweene a younger *Sachim*, Miantunnômu, and an elder *Sachim*, Caunoúnicus, of about foure score yeeres old, this young mans Uncle; and their agreement in the Government is remarkable:

The old *Sachim* will not be offended at what the young *Sachim* doth; and the young *Sachim* will not doe what hee conceives will displease his Uncle.

Saunèks

Saunks.	*The Queen, or Sachims Wife.*
Sauncksquûaog.	*Queenes.*
Otàn,-nash.	*The towne, townes.*
Otânick.	*To the towne.*
Sachimmaacómmock	*A Princes house,* which

according to their condition, is farre different from the other house, both in capacity or receit; and also the finenesse and quality of their Mats.

Ataúskawaw-wáuog.	*Lord, Lords.*
Wauôntam.	*A Wise man or Counsellour.*
Wauóntakick.	*Wise men.*
Enàtch *or* eàtch Keèn anawáyean.	*Your will shall be law.*
Enàtch neèn ánowa.	*Let my word stand.*
Ntínnume.	*He is my man.*
Ntacquêtunck ewò.	*He is my subject.*
Kuttáckquêtous.	*I will subject to you.*

Obs. Beside their generall subjection to the highest *Sachims,* to whom they carry presents: They have also particular Protectors, under *Sachims,* to whom they also carry presents, and upon any injury received , and complaint made, these Protectors will revenge it.

Ntannôtam.	*I will revenge it.*
Kuttannótous.	*I will revenge you.*
	Miâwene.

Miâwene.	*A Court or meeting.*
Wèpe cummiâwene.	*Come to the meeting.*
Miawêtuck.	*Let us meet.*
Wauwháutowash.	*Call a meeting.*
Miawêmucks.	*At a meeting.*
Miawéhettit.	*When they meet.*

Obs. The *Sachims*, although they have an absolute Monarchie over the people; yet they will not conclude of ought that concernes all, either Lawes, or Subsides, or warres, unto which the people are averse, and by gentle perswasion cannot be brought.

Peyaùtch naûgum.	*Let himselfe come here.*
Pétiteatch.	*Let him come.*
Mishaúntowash.	*Speake out.*
Nanántowash.	*Speake plaine.*
Kunnadsíttamen wèpe.	*You must inquire after this.*
Wunnadsittamútta.	*Let us seach into it.*
Neen pitch-nnadsítta-men.	*I will inquire into it.*
Machíssu ewò.	*He is naught.*
Cuttiantacompáw-wem.	*You are a lying fellow.*
Cuttiantakiskquâw-quaw.	*You are a lying woman.*
Wèpe cukkúmmoot.	*You have stole.*
Mat méshnawmônash	*I did not see those things* Màt

| Màt mèsh nummám menash. | *I did not take them.* |
| Wèpe kunnishquêko cummiskissawwaw. | *You are fierce and quarrelsome.* |

Obs. I could never discerne that excesse of scandalous sins amongst them, which *Europe* aboundeth with. Drunkennesse and gluttony, generally they know not what sinnes they be; and although they have not so much to re-straine them (both in respect of knowledge of God and Lawes of men) as the *English* have, yet a man shall never heare of such crimes amongst them of robberies, murthers, adulteries &c. as amongst the *English:* I conceive that the glorious Sunne of so much truth as shines in *England*, hardens our *English* hearts; for what the Sunne softeneth not, it hardens.

Tawhìtch yò enêan?	*Why doe you so?*
Tawhìtch cummoo-tóan?	*Why doe you steale?*
Tawhìtch nanompa-niêan?	*Why are you thus idle or base?*
Wewhepapúnnoke.	*Bind him.*
Wèpe kunnishaûmis.	*You kild him.*
Wèpe kukkeminean-tín.	*You are the murtherer.*
Sasaumitaúwhitch.	*Let him be whipt.*
Upponckquittáúw-hitch.	*Let him be imprisoned.*
	Níppitch

Níppitch ewò.	*Let him die.*
Níphéttitch.	*Let them die.*
Nìss-Nissòke.	*Kill him.*
Púm-púmmoke.	*Shoot him.*

Obs. The most usuall Custome amongst *th*em in executing punishments, is for the *Sachim* either to beat, or whip, or put to death with his owne hand, to which the common sort most quietly submit : though sometimes the *Sachim* sends a secret Executioner, one of his chiefest Warriours to fetch of a head, by some sudden unexpected blow of a Hatchet, when they have feared Mutiny by publike execution.

Kukkeechequaû-benitch.	*You shall be hanged.*
Níppansínnea.	*I am innocent.*
Uppansìnea-ewo.	*He is innocent.*
Matmeshnowaû-won.	*I knew nothing of it.*
NNnowaûntum.	*I am sorry.*
Nummachiemè.	*I have done ill.*
Aumaúnemoke.	*Let it passe, or take*
Konkeeteatch	*away this accusation.*
Ewó.	*Let him live.*
Konkeeteáhetti	*Let them live.*

Obser-

Observation generall, of their
        Government.

The wildest of the sonnes of Men have e-
ver found a necessity , (for preservation of
themselves, their Families and Properties)
to cast themselves into some Mould or forme
of Government.

        More particular:

Adulteries, Murthers, Robberies, Thefts,
    1   *Wild* Indians *punish these!*
And hold the Scales of Iustice so,
        That no man farthing leese.

When Indians *heare the horrid filths,*
    2   *Of* Irish, English *Men,*
The horrid Oaths and Murthers late,
        Thus say these Indians *then.*

We weare no Cloaths, have many Gods,
        And yet our sinnes are lesse:
You are Barbarians, Pagans wild,
        Your Land's the Wildernesse.

                    L   Chap. XIII.

Chap. XXIII.

Of *Marriage*.

VVUskéne.	*A young man.*
Keegsquaw.	*A Virgin or Maide.*
Segaûo.	*A Widdower.*
Segoúsquaw.	*A Widdow.*
Wussénetam.	*He goes a wooing.*
Nosénemuck.	*He is my sonne in Law.*
Wussenetûock,	*They make a match.*
Awetawátuock.	

Obs. Single fornication they count no sin, but after Mariage (which they solemnize by consent of Parents and publique approbation publiquely) then they count it hainous fer either of them to befalse.

Mammaûsu.	*An adulterer.*
Nummam mógwun-ewò.	*He hath wronged my bed.*
Pallè nochisquaûaw.	*He or She hath committed adultery.*

Obs. In this case the wronged party may put away or keepe the party offending: commonly, if the Woman be false, the offended Husband will be solemnely revenged upon the

the offendor, before many witnesses, by many blowes and wounds, and if it be to Death, yet the guilty resists not, nor is his Death revenged.

Nquittócaw.	*He hath one Wife.*
Neesócaw.	*He hath two Wives.*
Sshócowaw.	*He hath three.*
Yócowaw.	*Foure Wives, &c.*

Their number is not stinted, yet the chief Nation in the Country, the Narrigansets (generally) have but one Wife.

Two causes they generally alledge for their many Wives.

First desire of Riches, because the Women bring in all the increase of the Field, &c. the Husband onely fisheth, hunteth, &c.

Scecondly, their long sequestring themselves from their wives after conception, untill the child be weaned, which with some is long after a yeare old, generally they keep their children long at the breast:

Commíttamus.	*Your Wife.*
Cowéewo.	
Tahanawátu? ta shin-commaugemus.	*How much gave you for her?*
Napannetashom paûgatash	*Five fathome of their Money.*
Qutta, énada shoá-	*Six, or seven, or eight*

sûck

súck ta shompaú- gatash.	*Fathome.*

If some great mans Daughter *Piuckquom-paúgatash,* ten fathome.

Obs. Generally the Husband gives these payments for a Dowrie, (as it was in *Israell*) to the Father or Mother, or guardian of the Maide. To this purpose if the man be poore, his Friends and neighbours doe *pummanùm-minteàuguash,* that is contribute Money toward the Dowrie.

Nummíttamus.	*My Wife.*
Nullógana.	
Waumaûsu.	*Loving.*
Wunnêkesu.	*Proper.*
Maânsu.	*Sober and chast.*
Muchickéhea.	*Fruifull.*
Cutchashekeâmis?	*How many children have you had?*
Nquittékea.	*I have had one.*
Neesékea.	*Two, &c.*

Obs. They commonly abound with Children , and increase mightily ; except the plauge fall amongst them or other lesser sicknesses, and then having no meanes of recovery, they perish wonderfully.

Katoû eneéchaw.	*She is falling into Travell.*

Néechaw

Néechaw.	*She is in Travell.*
Paugcótche nechaú-waw.	*She is already deli-vered.*
Kitummâyi-mes-né-chaw.	*She was just now deli-vered.*

Obs. It hath pleased God in wonderfull manner to moderate that curse of the sorrowes of Child-bearing to these poore Indian Women: So that ordinaríly they have a wonderfull more speedy and easie Travell, and delivery then the Women of *Europe:* not that I thinke God is more gracious to them above other Women, but that it followes, First from the hardnesse of their constitution, in which respect they beare their sorrowes the easier.

Secondly from their extraordinary great labour (even above the labour of men) as in the Field, they sustaine the labour of it, in carrying of mighty Burthens , in digging clammes and getting other Shelfish from the Sea, in beating all their corne in Morters: &c. Most of them count it a shame for a Woman in Travell to make complaint, and many of them are scarcely heard to groane. I have often knowne in one Quarter of an houre a Woman merry in the House, and delivered and merry againe: aud within two

L 3   dayes

dayes abroad, and after foure or five dayes at worke, &c.

Noosâwwaw.	*A Nurse.*
Noònsu Nonánnis.	*A sucking Child* :
Wunnunògan.	*A Breast.*
Wunnunnóganash.	*Breasts.*
Munnúnnug.	*Milke.*
Aumáúnemun.	*To take from the breast,* *or Weane.*

Obs. They put away (as in Israell) frequently for other occasions beside Adultery, yet I know many Couples that have lived twenty, thirty, forty yeares together.

Npakétam.	*I will put her away.*
Npakénaqun.	*I am put away.*
Aquiepakétash.	*Doe not put away.*
Aquiepokesháttous	*Doe not break the knot*
Awetawátuonck.	*of Marriage.*
Tackquiũwock.	*Twins.*
Towiû-ûwock.	*Orphans.*
Ntouwiú.	*I am an Orphane.*
Wáuchaũnat.	*A Guardian.*
Wauchaúamachick.	*Guardians.*
Nullóquaso.	*My charge or Pupill,* *or Ward.*
Peewaúqun.	*Looke well to him &c.*

Generall

Generall Observations *of their*
Mariage.

God hath planted in the Hearts of the
Wildest of the sonnes of Men, an High
and Honourable esteeme of the Mariage bed,
insomuch that they universally submit unto
it, and hold the Violation of that Bed, Abo-
minable, and accordingly reape the Fruit
thereof in the abundant increase of posterity.

More Particular:

When Indians heare that some there are,
  (That Men the Papists call)
Forbidding Mariage Bed and yet,
  To thousand VVhoredomes fall:

They aske if such doe goe in Cloaths,
  And whether God they know?
And when they heare they're richly clad,
  know God, yet practice so.

No sure they're Beasts not men (say they,)
  Mens shame and soule disgrace,
Or men have mixt with Beasts and so,
  brought forth that monstrous Race.

L 4   CHAP. VII.

CHAP. XXIV.

Concerning their Coyne.

THe *Indians* are ignorant of *Europes* Coyne; yet they have given a name to ours, and call it *Monĕash* from the *English* Money.

Their owne is of two sorts; one white, which they make of the stem or stocke of the *Periwincle*, which they call Meteaûhock, when all the shell is broken off: and of this sort six of their small Beads (which they make with holes to string the bracelets) are currant with the *English* for a peny.

The second is black, incling to blew, which is made of the shell of a fish, which some *English* call *Hens*, Poquaûhock, and of this sort three make an *English* peny.

They that live upon the Sea side, generally make of it, and as many make as will.

The *Indians* bring downe all their sorts of Furs, which they take in the Countrey, both to the *Indians* and to the *English* for this *Indian* Money : this Money the *English*, *French* and *Dutch*, trade to the *Indians*, six hundred miles in severall parts (North and South from *New-*

England

England) for their Furres, and whatsoever
they stand in need of from them: as Corne,
Venison, &c.

Nquittómpscat.	1 *peny.*
Neesaúmscat.	2 *pence.*
Shwaúmscat.	3 *pence.*
Yowómscat.	4 *pence.*
Napannetashaúmscat.	5 *pence.*
Quttatashaúmscat, *or,* quttauatu.	6 *pence.*
Enadatashaúmscat.	7 *pence.*
Shwoasuck tashaúms-cat.	8 *pence.*
Paskugittashaúmscat.	9 *pence.*
Piuckquaúmscat.	10 *pence.*
Piuckquaúmscat nab naqùit.	11 *pence.*
Piuckquaúmscat nab nèes, &c.	12 *pence.*

Obs. This they call *Neèn,* which is two of
their *Quttáuatues,* or six pence.

Piukquaúmscat nab nashoàsuck, *which they call* Shwìn.	18$^{d.}$ 3 quttáuatues.
Neesneecheckaúmscat nab yòh, *or,* yowin.	2$^{s.}$ 4 quttáuatues.
Shwinchékaúmscat, *or* napannetashin.	2$^{s.}$ 6$^{d.}$ 5 quttáuatues.

Shwin-

Shwinchekaúmscat	2^s· 6^d· 6 quttáuatues.
Yowinnchekaúmscat nab neèse.	3^s· 6^d· 7 quttáuatues.
Yowinncheckaúmscat nabnashòasuck.	4^s· 8 quttáuatues.
Napannetashwincheckáumscat nab yòh.	4^s· 6^d· 9 quttáuatues
Quttatashincheck aumscat, *or, more commonly used* Piúckquat.	5^s· 10 quttaúatues, *or,* 10 six pences.

Obs. This *Piúckquat* being sixtie pence, they call *Nquittómpeg,* or *nquitnishcāusu,* that is, one fathom, 5 shillings.

This one fathom of this their stringed money, now worth of the English but five shillings (sometimes more) some few yeeres since was worth nine, and sometimes ten shillings *per* Fathome: the fall is occasioned by the fall of Beaver in *England:* the Natives are very impatient, when for English commodities they pay so much more of their money, and not understanding the cause of it; and many say the English cheat and deceive them, though I have laboured to make them understand the reason of it.

Neesaump-

Neesaumpaúgatuck,	10 shil. 2 Fathom.
Shwaumpáugatuck.	15 shil. 3 Fathom.
Yowompáugatuck, &c.	20 shil. 4 Fathom.
Piuckquampáugatuck *or*, Nquit pâusck.	50 shil. 10 Fathome.
Neespausuckquompáugatuck.	5 lib' 20 Fathome.
Shwepaûsuck.	30 Fathome.
Yowe paûsuck, &c.	
Nquittemittannauganompáugatuck.	40 Fathome, *or*, 10. pounds.
Neesemittannug, &c.	
Tashincheckompáugatuck?	*How many* Fathom?

Obs. Their white they call *Wompam* (which signifies white): their black *Suckáuhock* (*Súcki* signifying blacke.)

Both amongst themselves; as also the English and Dutch, the blacke peny is two pence white; the blacke fathom double, or, two fathom of white.

Wepe kuttassawompatímmin.	*Change my money.*
Suckaúhock, nausaké-sachick.	*The blacke money.*

Wawômpegs,

Wauômpeg, *or* Wau-ompésichick-mêsim	*Give me white.*
Assawompatíttea.	*Come, let us change.*
Anâwsuck.	*Shells.*
Meteaûhock.	*The Periwinckle.*
Suckaùanaûsuck.	*The blacke Shells.*
Suckauaskéesaquash.	*The blacke eyes,* or

that part of the shel-fish called *Poquaûhock* (or Hens) broken out neere the eyes, of vvhich they make the blacke.

Puckwhéganash *&* Múcksuck.	*Awle blades.*
Papuckakíuash.	*Britle,* or *breaking,*

Which they desire to be hardened to a britle temper.

Obs. Before ever they had *Awle blades* from *Europe* they made shift to bore this their shell money with stone and so fell their trees with stone set in a wooden staff, and usedwoden *howes*: which some old & poore women (fearfull to leave the old tradition) use to this day.

Natouwómpitea.	*A Coyner* or *Minter.*
Nnanatouwómpi-teem.	*I cannot coyne.*
Natouwómpitees.	*Make money or Coyne.*
Puckhùmmin.	*To bore through.*
Puckwhegonnaûtick.	*The Awle blade sticks.*

Tutte-

Tutteputch anâwsin.	*To smooth them*, which
they doe on stones.	
Qussùck-anash.	*Stone, Stones.*
Cauómpsk.	*A Whetstone.*
Nickáutick.	*A kinde of wooden Pincers* or *Vice.*
Enomphómmin.	*To thread* or *string.*
Aconaqunnaûog.	*Thread the Beads.*
Enomphómmin.	*Thread,* or *string these.*
Enomphósachick.	*Strung ones.*
Sawhóog & Sawhósachick.	*Loose Beads.*
Naumpacoûin.	*To hang about the necke.*

Obs. They hang these strings of money about their necks and wrists; as also upon upon the necks and wrists of their wives and children.

Máchequoce. | *A Girdle:*   Which they make curiously of one two, three, foure, and five inches thicknesse and more, of this money which (sometimes to the value of ten pounds and more) they weare about their middle and as a scarfe about their shoulders and breasts.

Yea the Princes make rich Caps and Aprons(or small breeches) of these Beads thus curiously strung into many formes and figures: their blacke and white finely mixt together.   Observa-

Observations *generall of their* Coyne.

The Sonnes of men having lost their Maker, the true and onely Treasure, dig downe to the bowels of the earth for gold and silver ; yea, to the botome of the Sea, for shells of fishes, to make up a Treasure, which can never truly inrich nor satisfie.

More particular:

1 *The* Indians *prize not* English *gold,*
    N*or* English Indians *shell:*
Each in his place will passe for ought,
    What ere men buy or sell.

English *and* Indians *all passe hence,*
    To an eternall place,
VVhere shels nor finest gold's worth ought,
    VVhere nought's worth ought but Grace.

This Coyne the Indians *know not of,*
    VVho knowes how soone they may?
The English *knowing, prize it not,*
    But fling't like drosse away.

C H A P.

Chap. XXV.

Of buying and selling.

ANaqushaŭog, *or* Anaqushánchick	*Traders.*
Anaqushénto.	*Let us trade.*
Cúttasha ?	*Have you this or that?*
Cowachaúnum?	
Nítasha.	*I have.*
Nowachaŭnum.	
Nquénowhick.	*I want this, &c.*
Nowèkineam.	*I like this.*
Nummachinámmin.	*I doe not like.*
Máunetash nqué- nowhick.	*I want many things.*
Cuttattaúamish.	*I will buy this of you.*
Nummouanaquish.	*I come to buy.*
Mouanaqushaúog, Mouanaqushánchick.	*Chapmen.*

Obs. Amongst themselves they trade their Corne, skins, Coates, Venison, Fish, &c. and sometimes come ten or twenty in a Company to trade amongst the *English.*

They have some who follow onely making of Bowes, some Arrowes, some Dishes, and

(the

(the Women make all their earthen Vessells)
some follow fishing, some hunting: most on
the Sea-side make Money, and store up shells
in Summer against Winter whereof to make
their money.

Nummautanàqúsh.	*I have bought.*
Cummanóhamin?	*Have you bought?*
Cummanohamoùsh.	*I will buy of you.*
Nummautanóhamin.	*I have bought.*
Kunnauntatáuamish.	*I come to buy this.*
Comaunekunnúo ?	*Hove you any Cloth?*
Koppócki.	*Thick cloth.*
Wassáppi.	*Thin.*
Súckinuit.	*Black, or blackish.*
Míshquinuit.	*Red Cloth.*
Wómpinuit.	*White Cloath.*

Obs. They all generally prize a Mantle of
English or *Dutch* Cloth before their owne
wearing of Skins and Furres, because they are
warme enough and Lighter.

Wompeqũayi.	*Cloth inclining to white,*

Which they like not, but desire to have a
sad coulour without any whitish haires, suit-
ing with their owne naturall Temper, which
inclines to sadnesse.

Etouwawâyi.	*Wollie on both sides.*
Muckũcki.	*Bare without Wool.*

Cheche-

Chechéke maútsha.	*Long-lasting.*
Qúnnascat.	*Of a great breadth.*
Tióckquscat.	*Of little breadth.*
Wùss.	*The Edge or lift.*
Aumpácunnish.	*Open it.*
Tuttepácunnish.	*Fold it up.*
Mat Weshegga-núnno.	*There is no Wool on it.*
Tanógganish.	*Shake it.*
Wúskinuit.	*New Cloth.*
Tanócki, tanócksha.	*It is torne or rent.*
Eatawûs.	*It is Old.*
Quttaûnch	*Feele it.*
Audtà	*A paire of small breeches or Apron.*

Cuppàimish I will pay you, which is a word newly made from the *English* word pay.

Tahenaúatu?	*What price?*
Tummòck cummé-insh.	*I will pay you Beaver.*
Teaúguock Cum-méinsh.	*I will give you Money.*
Wauwunnégachick.	*Very good.*

Obs. They have great difference of their Coyne, as the *English* have: some that will not passe without Allowance, and some again made of a Counterfeit shell, and their very

M   blacke

black counterfeited by a Stone and other Materialls: yet I never knew any of them much
deceived, for their danger of being deceived
(in these things of Earth) makes them caute-
lous.

Cosaúmawem.	*You aske too much.*
Kuttíackqussaûwaw.	*You are very hard.*
Aquie iackqussaûme.	*Be not so hard.*
Aquie Wussaúmo-wash.	*Doe not aske so much.*
Tashin Commê-sim?	*How much shall I give you?*
Kutteaûg Commé-insh.	*I will give you your Money.*
Nkèke Comméinsh.	*I will give you an Otter.*
Coanombúqusse Kuttassokakómme.	*You have deceived me.*

Obs. Who ever deale or trade with them,
had need of Wisedome, Patience, and Faithfulnesse in dealing: for they frequently say
Cuppànnauem, you lye, *Cuttassokakómme,*
you deceive me.

Misquésu Kunúkkeke	*Your Otter is reddish.*
Yò aúwusse Wunnê-gin	*This is better.*
Yo chippaúatu.	*This is of another price.*
Augausaúatu.	*It is Cheap.*
Múchickaúatu.	*It is deare.*

Wuttun-

Wuttunnaúatu.	*It is worth it.*
Wunishaūnto.	*Let us agree.*
Aquie neesquttónck qussish.	*Doe not make adoe.*
Wuchè nquíttompscat.	*About a penny.*

They are are marvailous subtle in their Bargaines to save a penny: And very suspicious that *English* men labour to deceive them: Therefore they will beate all markets and try all places, and runne twenty thirty, yea, forty mile, and more, and lodge in the Woods, to save six pence.

Cummámmenash nitteaúguash?	*Will you have my Money?*
Nonânum.	*I cannot.*
Nòonshem.	
Tawhitch nonanum êan?	*Why can you not?*
macháge nkòckie.	*I get nothing.*
Tashaumskussayi commêsim?	*How many spans will you give me?*
Neesaumsqussáyi.	*Two spans.*
Shwaumscussáyi.	*Three spans.*
Yowompscussáyi.	*Foure Spans.*
Napannetashaumscussâyi.	*Five spans.*
Quttatashaumíkus Sáyi.	*Six spans.*

M 2   Enada

Endatashaumscussâyì.	*Seven spans.*
Enadatashaumskut-tonâyi.	*Seven spans.*
Cowénaweke.	*You are a rich man.*

Obs. They will often confesse for their own ends, that the English are richer and wiser and valianter then themselves; yet it is for their owne ends, and therefore they adde *Nanoŭe*, give me this or that, a disease which they are generally infected with: some more ingenuous, scorne it; but I have often seene an *Indian* with great quanties of money about him, beg a Knife of an English man, who happily hath had never a peny of money.

Akêtash-tamòke.	*Tell my money.*
Now ánnakese.	*I have mis-told.*
Cosaúmakese.	*You have told too much.*
Cunnoónakese.	*You have told too little.*
Shoo kekíneass.	*Looke here.*
Wunêtu nitteaûg.	*My money is very good.*
Mamattissuôg kutteaùquock.	*Your Beads are naught.*
Tashin mesh commaûg?	*How much have you given?*
Chichêgin.	*A Hatchet.*
Anáskunck.	*A Howe.*
Maumichémanege.	*A Needle.*
Cuttatuppaúnamum.	*Take a measure.*

Tatup-

Tatuppauntúhom- min.	*To weigh with scales.*
Tatuppauntúock.	*They are aweighing.*
Netâtup.	*It is allone.*
Kaukakíneamuck. Pebenochichauquâ- nick.	} *A Looking Glasse.*

Obs. It may be wondred what they do with Glasses, having no beautie but a swarfish colour, and no dressing but nakednesse; but pride appeares in any colour, and the meanest dresse: and besides generally the women paint their faces with all sorts of colours.

Cuminanohamó- gunna.	*They will buy it of you.*
Cuppittakúnnemous.	*Take your cloth againe.*
Cuppittakunnamì.	*Will you serve me so?*
Cosaumpeekúnne- mun.	*You have tore me off too little cloth.*
Cummachetannakún namous.	*I have torn it off for you.*
Tawhìtch cuppítta- kunamiêan?	*Why doe you turne it upon my hand?*
Kutchichêginash, kaukinne pokéshaas.	*Your Hatchets will be soone broken.*
Teâno wáskishaas.	*Soone gapt.*
Natouashóckquittea.	*A Smith.*
Kuttattaúamish aûke	*I would buy land of you.*

Tou

Tou núckquaque?	*How much?*
Wuchè wuttotânick Plantation.	*For a Towne,* or,
Nissékineam.	*I have no mind to seeke.*
Indiansuck sekineám- wock.	*The Indians are not willing.*
Noonapûock naûgum	*They want roome themselves.*
Cowetompátimmin.	*We are friends.*
Cummaugakéamish.	*I will give you land.*
Aquìe chenawaûsish.	*Be not churlish.*

Generall Observation *of* Trade.

O the infinite wisedome of the most holy wise *God,* who hath so advanced *Europe* above *America,* that there is not a sorry *Howe, Hatchet, Knife,* nor a rag of cloth in all *America,* but what comes over the dreadfull *Atlantick* Ocean from *Europe:* and yet that *Europe* be not proud, nor *America* discouraged. What treasures are hid in some parts of *America,* and in our *New English* parts, how have foule hands (in smoakie houses) the first handling of those Furres which are after worne upon the hands of Queens and heads of Princes?

More

More particular:

1 *Oft have I heard these* Indians *say,*
  These English *will deceive us.*
Of all that's ours, our lands and lives.
  In th' end they will bereave us.

2 *So say they, whatsoever they buy,*
  (*Though small*)*which shewes they're shie*
Of strangers, fearefull to be catcht
  By fraud, deceipt, or lie.

3 Indians *and* English *feare deceits,*
  Yet willing both to be
Deceiv'd and couzen'd of precious soule,
  Of heaven, Eternitie.

CHAP. XXVI.

Of *Debts and Trusting.*

NOónat. Noonamau-tuckquàwhe.	*I have not money enough Trust me.*
Kunnoonamaútuck quaush.	*I will owe it you.*

M 4   They

Obs. They are very desirous to come into debt, but then he that trusts them, must sustaine a twofold losse:

First, of his Commoditie.

Secondly, of his custome, as I have found by deare experience : Some are ingenuous, plaine hearted and honest; but the most never pay, unlesse a man follow them to their severall abodes, townes and houses, as I my selfe have been forc'd to doe, which hardship and travells it hath yet pleased God to sweeten with some experiences and some little gaine of Language.

Nonamautuckquahé ginash.	*Debts.*
Nosaumautackquá- whe.	*I am much in debt.*
Pitch nippáutowin.	*I will bring it you.*
Chenock naquómbeg cuppauútiin nitteaû- guash.	*When Will you bring mee my money?*
Kunnaúmpatous, Kukkeéskwhush.	*I will pay you.*
Keéskwhim teaug mésin.	*Pay me my money.*
Tawhítch peyáuyean	*Why doe you come?*
Nnádgecom.	*I come for debts.*
Machêtu.	*A poore man.*

Num-

Nummácheke.	*I am a poore man.*
Mesh nummaúch-nem.	*I have been sicke.*
Nowemacaûnash nit-teaùquash.	*I was faine to spend my money in my sicknesse.*

Obs. This is a common, and as (they think) most satisfying answer, that they have been sick: for in those times they give largely to the Priests, who then sometimes heales them by conjurations; and also they keepe open house for all to come to helpe to pray with them, unto whom also they give money.

Mat noteaûgo.	*I have no money.*
Kekíneash nippê-tunck.	*Looke here in my bag.*
Nummáche maúga-nash	*I have already paid.*
Mat coanaumwaû-mis.	*You have not kept your word.*
Kunnampatôwin keénowwin.	*You must pay it.*
Machàge wuttama-ûntam.	*He minds it not.*
Machàge wuttamma-untammôock.	*They take no care about paying.*
Michéme notamma-ûntam.	*I doe alwayes mind it.*

Mat

| Mat nickowêmen naûkocks. | *I cannot sleep in the night for it.* |

Generall Observations *of their debts.*

It is an universall Disease of folly in men to desire to enter into not onely necessary, but unnecessary and tormenting debts contrary to the command of the only wise God: Owe no thing to any man, but that you love each other.
    More particular:

I have heard ingenuous Indians *say,*
    In debts, they could not sleepe.
How far worse are such English *then,*
    Who love in debts to keepe?

If debts of pounds cause restlesse nights
    In trade with man and man,
How hard's that heart that millions owes
    To God, and yet sleepe can?

Debts paid, sleep's sweet, sins paid, death's
        sweet,
    Death's night then's turn'd to light;
Who dies in sinnes unpaid, that soule
    His light's eternall night.

C H A P .

Chap. XXVII.

Of *their Hunting*, &c.

VVEe shall not name over the severall sorts of Beasts which we named in the Chapter of Beasts.

The Natives hunt two wayes:

First, when they pursue their game (especially Deere, which is the generall and wonderfull plenteous hunting in the Countrey:) I say, they pursue in twentie, fortie, fiftie, yea, two or three hundred in a company, (as I have seene) when they drive the woods before them.

Secondly, They hunt by Traps of severall sorts, to which purpose, after they have obserued in Spring-time and Summer the haunt of the Deere, then about Harvest, they goe ten or twentie together, and sometimes more, and withall (if it be not too farre) wives and children also, where they build up little hunting houses of Barks and Rushes (not comparable to their dwelling houses) and so each man takes his bounds of two, three, or foure miles, where hee sets thirty, forty, or fiftie

Traps

Traps, and baits his Traps with that food
the Deere loves, and once in two dayes he
walks his round to view his Traps.

Ntauchaûmen.	*I goe to hunt.*
Ncáttiteam weeyoùs.	*I long for Venison.*
Auchaûtuck.	*Let us hunt.*
Nowetauchaûmen.	*I will hunt with you.*
Anúmwock.	*Dogs.*
Kemehétteas.	*Creepe.*
Pìtch nkemehétteem	*I will creepe.*
Pumm púmmoke.	*Shoote.*
Uppetetoûa.	*A man shot accidentally.*
Ntaumpauchaûmen.	*I come from hunting.*
Cutchashineánna?	*How many have you kild*
Nneesnneánna.	*I have kild two.*
Shwinneánna.	*Three.*
Nyowinneánna.	*Foure.*
Npiuckwinneánna.	*Ten, &c.*
Nneesneechecttash-inneanna.	*Twentie.*
Nummouashâwmen.	*I goe to set Traps.*
Apè hana.	*Trap, Traps.*
Asháppock.	*Hempe.*
Masaûnock.	*Flaxe.*
Wuskapéhana.	*New Traps.*
Eataúbana.	*Old Traps.*

Obs. They are very tender of their Traps
where they lie, and what comes at them; for
they

they say, the Deere (whom they conceive
have a Divine power in them) will soone
smell and be gone.

| Npunnowwáumen. | *I must goe to my Traps.* |
| Nummíshkommin. | *I have found a Deere*; |

Which sometimes they doe, taking a Wolfe
in the very act of his greedy prey, when sometimes (the Wolfe being greedy of his prey)
they kill him: sometimes the Wolfe having
glutted himselfe with the one halfe, leaves the
other for his next bait; but the glad *Indian*
finding of it, prevents him.

And that wee may see how true it is, that
all wild creatures, and many tame prey upon
the poore Deere (which are there in a right
Embleme of Gods persecuted, that is hunted
people, as I observed in the Chapter of Beasts
according to the old and true saying:

Imbelles Damæ quid nisi præda sumus?

To harmlesse *Roes* and *Does*,
    Both wilde and tame are foes.)

I remember how a poore Deere was long
hunted and chased by a Wolfe, at last (as their
manner is) after the chase of ten, it may be
more miles running, the stout Wolfe tired
out the nimble Deere, and seasing upon it,
                                        kill'd

kill'd: In the act of devouring his prey, two
English Swine, big with Pig, past by, assaulted
the Wolfe, drove him from his prey, and de-
voured so much of that poore Deere, as they
both surfeted and dyed that night.

The Wolfe is an Embleme of a fierce blood-
sucking persecutor.

The Swine of a covetous rooting world-
ling, both make a prey of the Lord Jesus in
his poore servants.

Ncummóotamúck qun natóqus.	*The Wolfe hath rob'd me.*

Obs. When a Deere is caught by the leg in
the Trap, sometimes there it lies a day together before the Indian come, and so lies a
pray to the ranging Wolfe, and other wild
Beasts (most commonly the Wolfe) who sea-
seth upon the Deere and robs the Indian (at
his first devouring) of neere halfe his prey,
and if the Indian come not the sooner, hee
makes a second greedie Meale, and leaves him
nothing but the bones, and the torne Deere-
skins, especially if he call some of his greedy Companions to his bloody banquet.

Upon this the *Indian* makes a falling trap
called *Sunnúckhig*, (with a great weight of
stones) and so sometimes knocks the Wolfe

on

on the head, with a gaineful Revenge, especially if it bee a blacke Wolfe, whose Skins
they greatly prize.

Nanówwussu.	*It is leane.*
Wauwunnockôo.	*It is fat.*
Weékan.	*It is sweet.*
Machemóqut.	*It smells ill.*
Anìt.	*It is putrified.*
Poquêsu.	*Halfe a Deere.*
Poskáttuck &	*A whole Deere.*
Missêsu.	
Kuttíomp.	
Paucottaúwat.	*A Buck.*
Wawúnnes.	*A young Buck.*
Qunnèke.	*A Doe.*
Aunàn.	*A Fawne.*
Moósqin.	
Yo asipaugon	*Thus thick of fat.*
Noónatch, or,	*I hunt Venison.*
attuck ntíyu.	
Mishánneke ntíyu	*I hunt a Squirrill.*
Paukunnawaw ntío.	*I hunt a Beare, &c.*
Wusséke.	*The hinder part of the*
	Deere.
Apome-ichàsh.	*Thigh: Thighes.*
Uppèke-quòck.	*Shoulder, shoulders:*
Wuskàn,	*A bone.*
Wussúckqun	*A taile.*

Awem-

Awemanìttin.	*Their Rutting time.*
Paushinùmmin.	*To divide.*
Paushinummauatíttea.	*Let us divide.*

This they doe when a Controversie falls
out, whose the Deere should bee.

Caúskashunck,	*The Deere skin.*

Obs. Púmpom: a tribute Skin when a
Deere (hunted by the Indians, or Wolves) is
kild in the water. This skin is carried to the
Sachim or Prince , within whose territory the
Deere was slaine.

Ntaumpowwushaumen.	I *come from hunting.*

Generall Observation *of their hunting.*

There is a blessing upon endeavour, even to
the wildest *Indians;* the sluggard rosts not that
which he tooke in hunting but the substance
of the diligent (either in earthly or heavenly
affaires) is precious, *Prov.* 25.

More particular:

Great pains in hunting th' Indians *Wild,*
   And eke the English *tame;*
Both take, in woods and forrests thicke,
   To get their precious game.

                          Pleasure

Pleasure and Profit, Honour false,
   (The wordl's great Trinitie)
Drive all men through all wayes, all, times,
   All weathers, wet and drie.

Pleasure and Profits Honour, sweet,
   Eternall, sure and true,
Laid up in God, with equall paines;
   Who seekes, who doth pursue?

Chap. XXVIII.

Of *their* Gaming, &c.

THeir *Games,* (like the *English*) are of two
   sorts; private and publike:
Private, and sometimes publike; A *Game*
like unto the *English* Cards; yet, in stead of
Cards they play with strong *Rushes.*

Secondly, they have a kinde of Dice which
are Plumb stones painted, which they cast in
a Tray, with a mighty noyse and sweating:
Their publique *Games* are solemnized with
the meeting of hundreds; sometimes thousands, and consist of many vanities, none of
which I durst ever be present at, that I might

N   not

not countenance and partake of their folly, after I once saw the evill of them.

Ahânu.	*Hee laughes.*
Tawhitchahánean.	*Why doe you laugh?*
Ahánuock.	*They are merry.*
Nippauochâumen.	*We are dancing.*
Pauochaûog.	*They are playing or dancing.*
Pauochaútowwin.	*A Bable to play with.*
Akésuog.	*They are at Cards,* or *telling of Rushes.*
Pissinnéganash.	*Their playing Rushes.*
Ntakésemin.	*I am atelling,* or *counting;*

for their play is a kind of Arithmatick.

Obs. The chiefe Gamesters amongst them much desire to make their Gods side with them in their Games (as our *English* Gamesters so farre also acknowledge God) therefore I have seene them keepe as a precious stone a piece of Thunderbolt, which is like unto a Chrystall, which they dig out of the ground under some tree. Thunder-smitten, and from this stone they have an opinon of successe, and I have not heard any of these prove losers, which I conceive may be *Satans* policie and Gods holy Justice to harden them for their not rising higher from the Thunderbolt, to the God that send or shoots it.

Ntaquìe

Ntaquìe akésamen.	*I will leave play.*
Nchikossimúnnash.	*I will burne my Rushes.*
Wunnaugon-hómmin	*To play at dice in their Tray.*
Asaûanash.	*The painted Plumbstones which they throw.*
Puttuckquapúonck.	*A Playing Arbour.*

Obs. This Arbour or Play house is made of long poles set in the earth, foure square, sixteen or twentie foot high, on which they hang great store of their stringed money, have great stakings, towne against towne, and two chosen out of the rest by course to play the *Game* at this kinde of Dice in the midst of all their Abettors, with great shouting and solemnity: beside, they have great meetings of foot-ball playing, onely in Summer, towne against towne, upon some broad sandy shoare, free from stones, or upon some soft heathie plot because of their naked feet at which they have great stakings, but seldome quarrell.

| Pasuckquakoho-waûog. | *They meet to foot-ball.* |
| Cukkúmmote wèpe. | *You steale*; As I have |

often told them in their gamings, and in their great losings (when they have staked and lost their money, clothes, house, corne, and themselves (if single persons) they will confesse it being weary of their lives, and ready to make away themselves, like many an *English* man: an Embleme of the horrour of conscience, which all poore sinners walk in at last, when they see what wofull games they have played in their life, and now find themselves eternall Beggars.

Keesaqúnnamun, Another kinde of solemne publike meeting, wherein they lie under the trees, in a kinde of Religious observation, and have a mixture of Devotions and sports: But their chiefest Idoll of all for sport and game, is (if their land be at peace) toward Harvest, when they set up a long house called *Qunnè-kamuck*. Which signifies *Long house*, sometimes an hundred, sometimes two hundred foot long upon a plaine neer the Court (which they call *Kittcickaüick*) where many thousands, men and women meet, where he that goes in danceth in the sight of all the rest; and is prepared with money, coats, small breeches, knifes, or what hee is able to reach to, and gives these things away to the poore, who yet must particularly beg and say, *Cowequetúmmous*, that is, *I beseech you:* which word (although there is not one common beggar amongst them) yet they will often use when their richest amongst them would fain obtain ought by gift.

Generall

Generall Observations *of their* Sports.

This life is a short minute, eternitie followes. On the improvement or dis-improve-
ment of this short minute, depends a joyfull
or dreadfull eternity; yet (which I tremble
to thinke of) how cheape is this invaluable
Jewell, and how many vaine inventions and
foolish pastimes have the sonnes of men in all
parts of the world found out, to passe time &
post over this short minute of life, untill like
some pleasant River they have past into *mare
mortuum,* the dead sea of eternall lamentation.

More particular:

1　*Our* English *Gamesters scorne to stake
　　Their clothes as* Indians *do,*
*Nor yet themselves, alas, yet both
　　Stake soules and lose them to.*

2　*O fearfull Games! the divell stakes
　　But Strawes and Toyes and Trash,*
*(For what is All, compar'd with Christ,
　　But**Dogs meat and Swines wash?*　* Phil. 3. 8.
σκύβαλα

3　*Man stakes his Iewell-darling soule,
　　(His owne most wretched foe)*
N 3　　　　　*Ventures*

Ventures, and loseth all in sport
At one most dreadfull throw.

Chap. XXIX.

Of *their* Warre, &c.

A Quène. Nanoúeshin, & Awêpu.	*Peace.* *A peaceable calme;* for *Awêpu* signifies a calme.
Chépewess, & Mishittâshin.	*A Northerne storme of warre,* as they witti-

ly speake, and which *Eugland* now wofully
feeles, untill the Lord Jesus chide the winds,
and rebuke the raging seas.

Nummusquântum.	*I am angry.*
Tawhitch musquaw-naméan?	*Why are you angry?*
Aquie musquántash.	*Cease from anger.*
Chachépissu, nish-qûetu.	*Fierce.*
Tawhitch chachepi-séttit nishquéhet-tit?	*Why are they fierce?*

Cummus-

Cummusquáuna-muck.	*He is angry with you.*
Matwaûog.	*Souldiers.*
Matwaûonck.	*A Battle.*
Cummusqnaúnamish	*I am angry with you.*
Cummusquawnamè?	*Are you angry with me?*
Miskisaûwaw.	*A quarrelsome fellow.*
Tawhítch niskqúe-kean?	*Why are you so fierce?*
Ntatakcómmuck qun ewò.	*He strucke mee.*
Nummokókunitch	*I am robbed.*
Ncheckéqunnitch.	
Mecaûtea.	*A fighter.*
Mecāuntítea.	*Let us fight.*
Mecaúnteass.	*Fight with him.*
Wepè cummécautch.	*You are a quarreller.*
Jûhettítea.	*Let us fight.*
Jûhetteke.	*Fight,* Which is the

word of incouragement which they use when they animate each other in warre; for they use their tongues in stead of drummes and trumpets.

Awaùn necáwni aum píasha?	*Who drew the first bow, or shot the first shot?*
Nippakétatunck.	*He shot first at me.*
Nummeshannántam	*I scorne, or take it indig-*
Nummayaôntam.	*nation.*

N 4   *Obs.* This

Obs. This is a common word, not only in warre, but in peace also (their spirits in naked bodies being as high and proud as men more gallant) from which sparkes of the lusts of pride and passion, begin the flame of their warres.

Whauwháutowaw ánowat.	*There is an Alarum.*
Wopwawnónckquat.	*An hubbub.*
Amaúmuwaw paúdsha.	*A Messenger is come.*
Keénomp Múckquomp }paûog	*Captaines*, or *Valiant men.*
Negonshâchick.	*Leaders.*
Kuttówonck.	*A Trumpet.*
Popowuttáhig.	*A Drumme.*

Obs. Not that they have such of their owne making; yet such they have from the *French*: and I have knowne a good Drumme made amongst them in imitation of the *English.*

Quaquawtatatteâug	*They traine.*
Machíppog.	*A Quiver.*
Caúquat -tash.	*Arrow, Arrowes.*
Onúttug.	*An halfe Moone in war.*
Péskcunck.	*A Gunne.*
Saûpuck.	*Powder.*
Mátit.	*Vnloden.*
Méchimu.	*Loden.*

Mechi-

Mechimúash.	*Lode it.*
Shóttash.	*Shot*; A made word

from us, though their Gunnes they have
from the *French*, and often sell many a score
to the *English*, when they are a little out of
frame or Kelter.

Pummenúmmin	*To contribute to the*
teáuquash.	*warres.*
Askwhítteass.	*Keep watch.*
Askwhitteâchick.	*The Guard.*
Askwhitteaûg.	*Is is the Guard.*

Obs. I once travelled (in a place conceived dangerous) with a great Prince, and his
Queene and Children in company, with a
Guard of neere two hundred, twentie, or thirtie fires were made every night for the Guard
(the Prince and Queene in the midst) and
Sentinells by course, as exact as in *Europe*;
and when we travelled through a place where
ambushes were suspected to lie, a speciall
Guard, like unto a Life-guard, compassed
(some neerer, some farther of) the King and
Queen, my selfe and some *English* with me.
They are very copious and patheticall in O-
rations to the people, to kindle a flame of
wrath, Valour or revenge from all the Common places which Commanders use to insist
on.

Wesássu.

Wesássu.	*Afraid.*
Cowésass.	*Are you afraid?*
Tawhitch wesáse-an?	*Why feare you?*
Manowêsass.	*I feare none.*
Kukkúshickquock.	*They feare you.*
Nosemitteúnckquock	*They fly from us.*
Onamatta cowaûta	*Let us pursue.*
Núckqusha.	*I feare him.*
Wussémo-wock.	*He flies, they flie.*
Npauchíppowem.	*I flie for succour.*
Keesaúname.	*Save me.*
Npúmmuck.	*I am shot.*
Chenawaûsu.	*Churlish.*
Waumaûsu.	*Loving.*
Tawhitch chenawaû sean?	*Why are you churlish?*
Aumánsk. Waukaunòsint.	*A Fort.*
Cupshitteaûg.	*They lie in the way.*
Aumanskitteaûg.	*They fortifie.*
Kekaúmwaw.	*A scorner or mocker.*
Nkekaûmuck ewò.	*He scornes me.*
Aquìe kekaúmowash.	*Doe not scorne.*

Obs. This mocking (between their great ones) is a great kindling of Warres amongst them: yet I have known some of their chiefest say, what should I hazard the lives of my

precious

precious Subjects , them and theirs to kindle
a Fire, which no man knowes how farre, and
how long it will burne, for the barking of a
Dog?

Sékineam.	*I have no mind to it.*
Nissékineug	*He likes not me.*
Nummánneug.	*He hates me.*
Sekinneauhettúock.	
Maninnewauhet-tuock.	*They hate each other.*
Nowetompátimmin Wetompâchick.	*We are Friends.* / *Friends.*
Nowepinnátimin.	*We joyne together.*
Nowepinnâchick.	*My Companions in War, or Associats.*
Nowechusettímmin.	*We are Confederates.*
Néchuse ewò	*This is my Associate.*
Wechusittûock.	*They joyne together.*
Nwéche kokkêwem.	*I will be mad with him.*
Chickaūta wêtu.	*An house fired.*

Once lodging in an Indian house full of people, the whole Company (Women especially) cryed out in apprehension that the Enemy had fired the House, being about midnight: The house was fired but not by an
Enemy: the men ran up on the house top,
and with their naked hands beat out the Fire:
One scorcht his leg, and suddenly after they
came

came into the house againe, undauntedly cut
his leg with a knife to let out the burnt blood.

Yo ánawhone	*There I am wounded.*
Missinnege	*A Captaine.*
Nummissinnàm ewo.	*This is my Captive.*
Waskeiûhettím-mitch.	*At beginning of the. fight.*
Nickqueintónck-quock	*They come against us.*
Nickqueintouôog.	*I will make Warre upon them.*
Nippauquanaũog.	*I will destroy them*
Queintauatíttea.	*Let us go against them.*
Kunnauntatauhuck-qun.	*He comes to kill you.*
Paúquana.	*There is a slaughter.*
Pequttôog paúqua-nan.	*The Pequts are slaine.*
Awaun Wuttúnnene?	*Who have the Victory.*
Tashittáwho?	*How many are slaine?*
Neestawho.	*Two are slaine?*
Piuckqunneánna.	*Ten are slaine.*

Obs. Their Warres are farre lesse bloudy,
and devouring then the cruell Warres of *Europe*; and seldome twenty slaine in a pitcht
field : partly because when they fight in a
wood every Tree is a Bucklar.

When they fight in a plaine, they fight
with

with leaping and dancing, that seldome an
Arrow hits , and when a man is wounded,
unlesse he that shot followes upon the wounded, they soone retire and save the wounded: and yet having no Swords, nor Guns, all
that are slaine are commonly slain with great
Valour and Courage : for the Conquerour
ventures into the thickest , and brings away
the Head of his Enemy.

Niss-níssoke.	*Kill kill.*
Kunnish	*I will kill you.*
Kunnìshickqun ewò.	*He will kill you.*
Kunníshickquock.	*They will kill you.*
Siuckissûog	*They are stout men.*
Nickummissûog	*They are Weake.*
Nnickummaunámaûog.	*I shall easily vanquish. them.*
Neene núppamen.	*I am dying?*
Cowaúnckamish.	*Quarter, quarter.*
Kunnanaumpasúmmish.	*Mercy, Mercy.*
Kekuttokaûntá,	*Let us parley.*
Aquétuck.	*Let us cease Armes.*
Wunnishaûnta.	*Let us agree.*
Cowammáunsh.	*I love you.*
Wunnétu ntá.	*My heart is true.*
Tuppaûntash.	*Consider what I say.*

Tuppaún-

Tuppaúntamoke.	*Doe you all consider.*
Cummequaùnum cummíttamussus- suck ká cummucki- aûg.	*Remember your Wives, and Children.*
Eatch kèen anawâye- an.	*Let all be as you saye.*
Cowawwunnaûwem.	*You speake truly.*
Cowauôntam.	*You are a wise man.*
Wetompátitea.	*Let us make Friends.*

Generall Observations *of their Warres.*

How dreadfull and yet how righteous is it with the most righteous Judge of the whole World, that all the generations of Men being turn'd Enemies against, and fighting against Him who gives them breath and Being, and all things, (whom yet they cannot reach) should stab, kill, burne, murther and devoure each other?

More Particular.

The Indians count of Men as Dogs,
   1 *It is no Wonder then:*
They teare out one anothers throats!
   But now that English *Men,*

                              That

That boast themselves Gods Children, and
   2 *Members of Christ to be,)*
That they should thus break out in flames.
      Sure 'tis a Mystery!

Rev. ⎱ *The second sea'ld Mystery or red* Horse,
2.6. ⎰   *Whose Rider hath power and will,*
      To take away Peace from Earthly Men,
      They must Each *other* kill.

Chap. XXX.

Of their paintings.

1. THey paint their Garments, &c.
2.   The men paint their Faces in
      Warre.
3. Both Men and Women for pride, &c.

Wómpi	*White.*
Mówi-súcki.	*Black.*
Msqùi.	*Red.*
Wesaûi	*Yellow.*
Askáski.	*Greene.*
Peshaûi.	*Blew, &c.*

Obs. Wunnàm their red painting which they
                                    most

most delight in, and is both the Barke of the
Pine, as also a red Earth.

Míshquock.	*Red Earth.*
Métewis.	*Black Earth.*

From this *Mètewis* is an Indian Towne a
day and a halfes Journey, or lesse (*West*,
from the *Massachusets*) called *Metewêmesick.*

Wussuckhòsu.	*A painted Coat.*

Of this and *Wússuckwheke*, (the English Letters, which comes neerest to their painting I
spake before in the Chapter of their clothing.

Aunakêsu.	*He is painted.*
Aunakéuck.	*They are painted.*
Tawhìtch auna kéan?	*Why doe you paint your selfe?*
Chéskhosh.	*Wipe off.*
Cummachiteoûwu- nash kuskeésuckquash.	*You spoile your Face.*
Mat pitch cowáhick Manìt keesiteónckqus	*The God that made you will not know you.*

Generall Observations of their paintings.

It hath been the foolish Custome of all
barbarous Nations to paint and figure their
Faces and Bodies (as it hath been to our shame
and griefe, wee may remember it of some of
our Fore-Fathers in this Nation.) How much
then are we bound to our most holy Maker

for

for so much knowledge of himselfe revealed in so much Civility and Piety? and how should we also long and endeavour that *América* may partake of our mercy:

More particular:

Truth is a Native, naked Beauty; but
    Lying Inventions are but Indian Paints,
2 *Dissembling heartstheir Beautie's but a Lye,*
Truth is the proper Beauty of Gods Saints.

Fowle are the Indians *Haire and painted Faces,*
  2 *More foule such Haire, such Face in* Israel.
England *so calls her selfe, yet there's*
    Absoloms *foule Haire and Face of* Jesabell.

Paints will not bide Christs washing Flames
    of fire,
    Fained Inventions will not bide such stormes:
O that we may prevent him, that betimes,
    Repentance Teares may wash of all such
    Formes.

CHAP. XXXI.

Of Sicknesse.

N Ummaŭchnem   *I am sick.*
  Mauchinaui.   *He is sick.*

O   Yo

Yo Wuttunsín	*He keepes his Bed.*
Achie nummauch-nem.	*I am very sick.*
Nóonshem metesím-min.	*I cannot eate.*
Mach ge nummete símmin.	*I eat nothing.*
Tocketussinámmin?	*What think you?*
Pitch nkéeteem?	*Shall I recover?*
Niskéesaqush mau-chinaash.	*My eyes faile me.*
Ncussawontapam.	*My head akes.*
Npummaumpiteunck	*My Teeth ake.*
Nchesammáttam, Nchésammam.	*I am in paine.*

Obs. In these cases their Misery appeares, that they have not (but what sometimes they get from the *English*) a raisin or currant or any physick, Fruit or spice , or any Comfort more than their Corne and Water, &c. In which bleeding case wanting all Meanes of recovery, or present refreshing I have been constrained to, and beyond my power to refresh them, and I beleeve to save many of them from Death,who I am confident perish many Millions of them (in that mighty continent) for want of Meanes.

| Nupaqqóntup | *Bind my head.* |
| Kúspissem. | Wauaúpunish |

Wauaúpunish Nippaquontup.	*Lift up my head.*
Nchésamam nséte.	*My Foot is sore.*
Machage nickow èmen	*I sleep not.*
Nnanótissu.	*I have a Feaver.*
Wàme kussópita nohock.	*My body burnes.*
Ntátupe nòte, or chíckot.	*I am all on fire.*
Yo ntéatchin.	*I shake for Cold.*
Ntátuppe wunnêpog.	*I shake as a leafe.*
Puttuckhumma.	*Cover me.*
Paútous nototam min.	*Reach me the drinke.*

Obs. Which is onely in all their extremities a little boild water, without the addition of crum or drop of other comfort : O *Englands* mercies, &c.

Tahaspunâyi?	*What ayles he?*
Tocketúspanem?	*What aile you?*
Tocketuspunnaúmaqūn?	*What hurt hath he done to you?*
Chassaqúnsin?	*How long hath he been sick?*
Nnanowwêteem	*I am going to visit.*

Obs. This is all their refreshing, the Visit

of Friends, and Neighbours, a poore empry
visit and presence, and yet indeed this is very solemne, unlesse it be in infectious diseases,
and then all forsake them aud flie, that I have
often seene a poore House left alone in the
wild Woods, all being fled, the living not
able to bury the dead: so terrible is the apprehension of an infectious disease, that not
only persons, but the Houses and the whole
Towne takes flight.

Nummòckquese.	*I have a swelling.*
Mocquêsui	*He is swelled.*
Wàme wuhòck- Mockquêsui.	*All his body is swelled.*
Mamaskishaûi.	*He hath the Pox.*
Mamaskishaûonck.	*The Pox.*
Mamaskishaûmitch.	*The last pox.*
Wesauashaûi.	*He hath the plague.*
Wesauashaûonck.	*The plague.*
Wesauashaûmitch.	*The great plague.*

Obs. Were it not that they live in sweet
Aire, and remove persons and Houses from
the infected, in ordinary course of subordi-
nate Causes, would few or any be left alive,
and surviving.

Nmunnádtommin.	*I vomit.*
Nqúnnuckquus.	*I am lame.*
Ncúpsa.	*I am deafe.*

Npóckunnum.

Npóckunnum.	*I am blind.*
Npockquanámmen.	*My disease is I know not what.*
Pésuponck.	*An Hot-house.*
Npesuppaûmen.	*I goe to sweate.*
Pesuppaûog.	*They are sweating.*

Obs. This Hot-house is a kind of little Cell or Cave, six or eight foot over, round, made on the side of a hill (commonly by some Rivulet or Brooke) into this frequently the men enter after they have exceedingly heated it with store of wood, laid upon an heape of stones in the midle. When they have taken out the fire, the stones keepe still a great heat: Ten, twelve, twenty more or lesse, enter at once starke naked, leaving their coats, small breeches (or aprons) at the doore, with one to keepe all: here doe they sit round these hot stones an houre or more, taking *Tobacco*, discoursing, and sweating together; which sweating they use for two ends: First, to cleanse their skin: Secondly, to purge their bodies, which doubtlesse is a great meanes of preserving them, and recovering them from diseases, especially from the *French* disease, which by sweating and some potions, they perfectly and speedily cure: when they come forth (which is matter of admiration) I have seene

O 3   them

them runne (Summer and Winter) into the Brooks to coole them, without the least hurt.

Misquineash.	*The vaines.*
Msqui, neépuck.	*Blood*
Nsanapaushaumen.	*I have the bloody Flixe.*
Matux puckqua- tchick aũwaw.	*He cannot goe to stool.*
Powwaw.	*Their Priest.*
Maunêtu.	*A Conjurer.*
Powwâw nippétea.	*The priest is curing him.*
Yo Wutteantawaw.	*He is acting his Cure.*

Obs. These Priests and Conjurers (like *Simon Magus*) doe bewitch the people, and not onely take their Money, but doe most certainly (by the help of the Divell) worke great Cures though most certaine it is that the greatest part of their Priests doe meerely abuse them and get their Money, in the times of their sicknesse, and to my knowledge, long for sick times: and to that end the poore people store up Money, and spend both Money and goods on the *Powwâws*, or Priests in these times, the poore people commonly dye under their hands, for alas, they administer nothing but howle and roare, and hollow over them, and begin the song to the rest of the People about them, who all joyne (like a Quire) in Prayer to their Gods for them.

Máskit

Máskit ponamíin.	*Give me a Plaister.*
Maskit	*Give me some physicke*
Cotatámhea.	*Drinke.*

Both which they earnestly desire of the *English,* and doe frequently send to my selfe, and others for, (having experimentally found some Mercy of that kind (through Gods blessing) from us.

| Nickeétem. | *I am recovered.* |
| Kitummâyi nick êekon. | *I am just now recovered.* |

Generall Observation *of their sicknesse.*

It pleaseth the most righteous, and yet patient God to warne and summon, to try and arraigne the universall race of *Adams* sonnes (commonly) upon Beds of sicknesse before he proceed to execution of Death and Judgement: Blessed those soules which prevent Judgement, Death and sicknesse to, and before the evill dayes come, Arraigne, and Judge themselves, and being sick for Love to Christ, find him or seek him in his Ordinances below, and get unfained Assurance of Eternall enjoyment of Him, when they are here no more.

O 4   more

More particular:

One step twix't Me and Death, (*twas*
                    Davids *speech,*)
  1 *And true of sick Folks all*:
Mans Leafe it fades, his Clay house cracks;
      Before it's dreadfull Fall.

Like Grashopper the Indian *leapes,*
  2 *Till blasts of sicknesse rise* :
Nor soule nor Body Physick hath,
      Then Soule and Body dies.

A happy English *who for both,*
      Have precious physicks store :
How should (*when Christ hath both refresh't,*
      Thy love and zeale be more ?

Chap. XXXII.

Of Death *and* Buriall, &c.

As Pummíssin. | *He is not yet departed.*
Neene. | *He is drawing on.*
Paúsawut kitonck- | *He cannot live long.*
quêwa.

Cheché-

Chachéwunnea.	*He is neere dead.*
Kitonckquêi.	*Hee is dead.*
Nipwì mâw.	*He is gone.*
Kakitonckquêban.	*They are dead and gone.*
Sequttôi.	*He is in blacke ;* That

is, He hath some dead in his house (whether
wife or child *&c.*) for although at the first being sicke, all the Women and Maides blacke
their faces with soote and other blackings;
yet upon the death of the sicke, the father, or
husband, and all his neighbours, the Men also (as the *English* weare blacke mourning
clothes) weare blacke *Faces,* and lay on soote
very thicke, which I have often seene clotted
with their teares.

This blacking and lamenting they observe
in most dolefull manner, divers weekes and
moneths; yea, a yeere, if the person be great
and publike.

Séqut.	*Soote.*
Michemeshâwi.	*He is gone for ever.*
Mat wònck kunnaw- mòne.	*You shall never see him more.*
Wunnowaúntam Wullóasin.	*Grieved and in bitter- nesse.*
Nnowántam,nlôasin.	*I am grieved for you.*

Obs. As they abound in lamentations for
the dead, so they abound in consolation to
the

the living, and visit them frequently, using this word *Kutchímmoke, Kutchímmoke,* Be of good cheere, which they expresse by stroaking the cheeke and head of the father or mother, husband or wife of the dead.

Chepassôtam.	*The dead Sachim.*
Mauchaúhom.	*The dead man.*
Mauchaûhomwock- Chepeck.	} *The dead.*
Chepasquâw.	*A dead woman.*
Yo ápapan.	*He that was here.*
Sachimaûpan.	*He that was Prince here.*

Obs. These expressions they use, because, they abhorre to mention the dead by name, and therefore, if any man beare the name of the dead he changeth his name; and if any stranger accidentally name him, he is checkt, and if any wilfully name him he is fined; and and amongst States, the naming of their dead *Sachims,* is one ground of their warres; so terrible is the King of Terrors, Death, to all naturall men.

Aquie míshash, aquie mishómmokc.	*Doe not name.*
Cowewênaki.	*You wrong mee,* to wit, *in naming my dead.*
Posakúnnamun.	*To bury.*

Aukùck

Aukùck pónamun. | *To lay in the earth.*
Wesquáubenan. | *To wrap up,* in winding
mats or coats, as we say, winding sheets.

Mockuttásuit, One of the chiefest esteeme,
who winds up and buries the dead, commonly some wife, grave, and well descended man
hath that office.

When they come to the Grave, they lay
the dead by the Grave's mouth, and then all
sit downe and lament, that I have seen teares
run downe the cheekes of stoutest Captaines,
as well as little children in abundance: and
after the dead is laid in Grave, and sometimes
(in some parts) some goods cast in with them,
They have then a second great lamentation,
and upon the Grave is spread the Mat that
the party died on, the Dish he eat in; and
sometimes a faire Coat of skin hung upon the
next tree to the Grave, which none will
touch, but suffer it there to rot with the
dead: Yea, I saw with mine owne eyes that
at my late comming forth of the Countrey,
the chiefe and most aged peaceable Father of
the Countrey, *Caunoūnicus,* having buried his
sonne, he burn'd his owne Palace, and all his
goods in it, (amongst them to a great value)
in a sollemne remembrance of his sonne, and
in a kind of humble Expiation to the Gods,
who

who (as they believe) had taken his sonne
from him.

The generall Observation *of their* Dead.

O, how terrible is the looke the speedy
and serious thought of death to all the sons
of men? Thrice happy those who are dead
and risen with the Sonne of God, for they
are past from death to life, and shall not see
death (a heavenly sweet Paradox or Ridle)
as the Son of God hath promised them.

More particular:

The Indians *say their bodies die,*
  Their soules they doe not die;
Worse are then Indians *such, as hold*
  The soules mortalitie.

Our hopelesse Bodie rots, say they,
  Is gone eternally,
English *hope better, yet some's hope*
  Proves endlesse miserie.

Two Worlds of men shall rise and stand
  'Fore Christs most dreadfull barre;
Indians, *and* English *naked too,*
  That now most gallant are.

                                    True

True Christ most Glorious then shall make
  New Earth, and Heavens New;
False Christs, false Christians then shall quake,
  O blessed then the True.

Now, to the most High and most Holy, Immortall, Invisible, and onely Wise God, who alone is *Alpha* and *Omega*, the *Beginning* and the *Ending*, the *First* and the *Last*, who *Was* and *Is*, and is to *Come*; from *Whom*, by *Whom*, and to *Whom* are all things; by *Whose* gracious assistance and wonderfull supportment in so many varieties of hardship and outward miseries, I have had such converse with Barbarous Nations, and have been mercifully assisted, to frame this poore K E Y, which may, (through His Blessing) in His owne holy season) open a Doore; yea, Doors of unknowne Mercies to Us and Them, be Honour, Glory, Power, Riches, Wisdome, Goodnesse and Dominion ascribed by all His in Jesus Christ to Eternity, *Amen.*

F I N I S .

The TABLE.

XX. Of

The TABLE.

I have further treated of these *Natives* of *New-England*, and that great point of their *Conversion* in a little additionall *Discourse* apart from this.

I Have read over these thirty *Chapters of the* American Language, *to me wholly uuknowne, and the* Observations, *these I conceive inoffensive; and that the Worke may conduce to the happy end intended by the* Author.

Io. LANGLEY.

Printed according to this Licence; and entred into *Stationers Hall.*

COSIMO is a specialty publisher of books and publications that inspire, inform, and engage readers. Our mission is to offer unique books to niche audiences around the world.

COSIMO BOOKS publishes books and publications for innovative authors, nonprofit organizations, and businesses. **COSIMO BOOKS** specializes in bringing books back into print, publishing new books quickly and effectively, and making these publications available to readers around the world.

COSIMO CLASSICS offers a collection of distinctive titles by the great authors and thinkers throughout the ages. At **COSIMO CLASSICS** timeless works find new life as affordable books, covering a variety of subjects including: Business, Economics, History, Personal Development, Philosophy, Religion & Spirituality, and much more!

COSIMO REPORTS publishes public reports that affect your world, from global trends to the economy, and from health to geopolitics.

CPSIA information can be obtained
at www.ICGtesting.com
Printed in the USA
BVOW08s0924210617
487487BV00001B/20/P